MILLENNIUM:
Fears, Fantasies & Facts

MILLENNIUM

Fears, Fantasies & Facts

Astrologers Predict

2000

Foreword by Marion D. March

Cover and book design by Daryl S. Fuller

International Standard Book Number 0-935127-62-3

Published by ACS Publications
5521 Ruffin Road
San Diego, California 92123-1314
www.astrocom.com

First Printing March 1998
Second Printing March 1999

FOREWORD

What a lovely name "Millennium" - it's so melodious, so foreign and elegant sounding. Rarely used, (like every 1000 years or so) it's easily misspelled. But why, oh why, does such a lovely word inspire such fear or dark thoughts in so many minds? When I read predictions or prognostications for the future, it sounds like doomsday is ready to arrive. Whatever catastrophe can possibly happen - we'll experience it, maybe not in the year 2000, but beware of 2001 and watch out for 2002! You would think that we were all a bunch of illiterates, totally imbued with superstition.

Yet, the last time I looked, most astrologers I know seem very literate, very knowledgeable and quite erudite. So what possesses so many of them to think that three zeros at the end of a two will make a difference in the scheme of things? After all, we know that dates and calendars are man-made, and have been changed quite a few times in the past. Most astrologers struggle with the changes from the Julian Calendar in the 16th century to the Gregorian one we use now. Some countries like Russia still have not made the change in all their smaller towns and villages. So who knows what year it is to them! Of course the Chinese celebrate a totally different year, as do Orthodox Jews.

But leave it up to us, the so-called "reasonable" people, to react like scared rabbits. To me it seems that as a community, we are falling into the same syndrome that befalls newspapers — only "bad" news sells, so lets print all failures, murders, robberies and weather catastrophes, because it is too boring to read about kindness, friendship, minor success stories and small daily acts of heroism. We would rather forecast floods, riots and upheaval than peace or a good economy.

"Now come on Marion," say my colleagues, "Are you becoming a romantic sentimentalist? Just look at some of the aspects, look at Edgar Cayce's prophecy about the shifting of the poles, and even better yet, Nostradamus' famous quatrain about Taurus/May and a major earthquake." Well, Nostradamus is probably the main reason why I pay little attention to famous or infamous predictions. I've heard about that particular one since I got married (1948) and my mother in law, a great Nostradamus follower, informed me that I was taking her son into pretty certain death by moving from Switzerland to California. She had the definite date, May 25, 1950 and I had to promise her that we would not be in California at that time. On our next Europe visit I received a revised date, May 21, 1963. In 1969 she gave me "the most absolute date ever, confirmed by all Nostradamus experts." I carefully posted it from year to year into my *Celestial Guide*: July 15, 1983 at 2:30 am — there would be 18 million dead!

Well, so much for predictions. What about some interesting up and coming dates? Quite a few people are talking about "that terrible eclipse on August 11, 1999 - the one where we have a fixed grand cross....." Now I'll let you interpret all the disasters that can, could, will or should happen then. Yes, there are some difficult aspects and not too much relief, except the Venus/Saturn trine; but if you look back, there have been so many eclipses with more stressful aspects and yet here we are, entering the next millennium. The same dire prognostication could be made for May 3, 2000 when seven of the planets, all but the three transcendentals, are in Taurus.

But we weathered that same array of planets when they were in Pisces in 1762, and at that time Pluto and Neptune had not been discovered and Uranus was barely known. I can just visualize how freaked out astrologers were. Closer to the present, in January 1994 seven planets were in Capricorn — and in Steven Sondheim's immortal words "But we're still here!"

If an acorn falls on your head, you know it's not the whole sky falling! Remember Franklin Delano Roosevelt's quote: "We have nothing to fear but fear itself." Live the future accordingly.

Marion D. March
December 22, 1997

Table of Contents

Kim Rogers Gallagher

Maritha Pottenger

Introduction

As the completion of a set of one thousand years draw near, fears and fantasies about what the "new millennium" will hold are rampant. This book is our contribution to shedding the light of a few facts into this area—along with projections based on physics, political and social trends, astrological analysis, demographics, and the odds-makers in our society.

Marion March offers an upbeat foreword which looks back at Nostradamus and our history while pointing to the hopes we can have for the future. She provides a realistic perspective and sensible framework within which we can view competing ideas about the millennium.

Maritha Pottenger explores some of the specific scenarios offered by various prophets—from meteor strikes to alien invasions; from major Earth changes to global warming; from pestilences and plagues to Armageddon; from economic collapse to religious wars; from World War III to a new golden age of peace, love, and harmony. She discusses the likelihood of each of the different possibilities being offered. She closes with an examination of the horoscopes for 2000 and 2001 and some specific predictions about what those years have to offer.

Zipporah Dobyns provides a historical overview for the reader. She traces the connections between the patterns in the sky and events on Earth back thousands of years. She discusses different calendar systems and notes the arbitrary nature of the demarcation which is anticipated with anxiety and with glee. Dr. Dobyns explains how many of the myths of one age ending (or one civilization being destroyed—often beneath the waves) are related to the astronomical phenomenon of precession of the equinoxes. She looks at some of the past and current apocalyptic religious beliefs and how they tend to increase during periods of intense stress. She points out how a too-literal interpretation of ancient myths has led to much needless concern.

Maria Kay Simms traces the concept of a "new age" through history. Using the framework of the zodiacal ages (popularized in the "Age of Aquarius" song), she discusses some of the patterns of history—and looks ahead to possible and probable futures. Maria Simms explores how people are making a core redefinition of God—moving from an external source of power to an internal one. As she traces the evolution of humanity's relationship to the divine, she discusses the timing of the (still distant) Age of Aquarius and what it is likely to mean for humanity. She clarifies the timing of the astrological ages and discusses some of the ramifications of the term "New Age."

Kim Rogers-Gallagher, in her inimitable style (full of Sagittarian humor) explores likely trends for the next 1000 years. Kim's article has a great introduction to what astrology is and how to use it in looking at world events. (Some readers may prefer to begin here.) She projects developments in politics, fashion, communication, technology, geography, human relationships, and much more. In addition to looking at the big picture, she compares the horoscope for the New Millennium to the horoscope of the United States and offers some specific predictions for America—and for the rest of the world. She shows us both the darkness and the light which are possible, and encourages us to focus on the best possibilities which lie before us.

All five authors emphasize common sense, logic, and doing what one can to make the most of challenges. **All five offer suggestions regarding steps each individual person (and humanity) can take to improve the probable future.** This book focuses on practicality, hope, sorting through competing pictures of disaster and identifying what is worth worrying about—and what is not. It is our hope that it will be a beacon of inspiration amidst much literature which has been excessively pessimistic. We wish all our readers the best in preparing for the New Millennium!

WHAT CAN WE EXPECT AFTER 2000?

In the year 2000 and beyond, we can expect one or more of the following scenarios to occur. Which one(s) do you suspect? Cast your vote and read on for more data!

Scenarios for Beyond 2000 A.D.

- A major meteor strikes the Earth. The resultant climatic changes kill most of the Earth's population.

- Aliens invade and take over all governments.

- The Earth flips anywhere from 20 to 180 degrees. Millions die instantly; many more slowly as their environment shifts radically. (This is variously ascribed to the ice on the poles getting out of balance or shifts in the Earth's magnetic field.)

- Armageddon occurs. The Anti-Christ tries to take over the world. The forces of God and the Devil clash mightily. The powers of Heaven win out, but Earth is destroyed. The few faithful and chosen are taken away to Heaven.

- Global warming becomes a serious problem sooner than people expect. Sunscreen becomes required at all times. The Earth heats up. Prime agricultural areas are hit hard which leads to economic, social, and political unrest.

- California falls into the ocean—or is buried under immense tidal waves.

- Weather extremes (in terms of tornadoes, hurricanes, volcanoes, etc.) become commonplace.

- New, more deadly pestilences develop and spread rapidly throughout the world.

- Tribalism rises in force and each small group begins fighting against every other small group.

- Religious fanticism rises. Intolerance and hate crimes become endemic and common.

- A worldwide depression strikes. The Stock Markets collapse and economic ruin stares many people in the face.

- Spiritual evolution causes a radical shift in consciousness among a critical mass of people. A new golden age of peace, light, and harmony begins.

- World War III begins, probably triggered by events in the Near East.

The popular literature of our time is full of terrifying prophecies. Some people are expecting Armageddon (the final battle between good and evil) ending with the destruction of the Earth. Others are predicting a "polar flip" so that major climactic disasters result. (The work of both Edgar Cayce and Ruth Montgomery is being interpreted as predicting an axis shift before 2001.) The one being predicted now will, it is assumed, generate thousand-foot tidal waves, destroying coastal areas and traveling far inland. These Earth changes would cause California to be buried under the ocean (and Arizona to develop some beach front property). New polar areas would quickly become sub-zero and people would freeze. Volcanoes would be triggered all over the world. Winds would be whipped up and cause massive havoc. Our interdependent world would be devastated with transportation difficult and consequent starvation, freezing, etc., due to lack of food, fuel, and basic necessities. Authors of such views paint a very terrifying picture.

Comets are associated with disasters in much literature. We've already seen the suicide of the Heaven's Gate people associated with the Comet Hale-Bopp. One view of Nostradamus has him predicting a comet in August of 1999 which will strike the Atlantic Ocean, kill billions of people and bring on a nuclear winter. A Saint Hildegard (in the 12th century) predicted a comet around this turning of the century which would devastate a great nation with earthquakes, storms and waves of water.

Various American Indian sources are said to point to a coming apocalypse—ranging from Black Elk and Crazy Horse reputed to have predicted three world wars within four generations, to the Hopi view of a "Great Purification" to come to the supposed ending of the Mayan calendar. (Some translators of Nostradamus interpret certain quatrains as implying a World War III as well.) Dannion Brinkley, who returned to life after a near-death experience of 28 minutes, has made several predictions about the probable future (unless we change our ways for the better). His scenarios include World War III with nuclear and chemical weapons, the economic collapse of the United States, devastating earthquakes, and people starving to death in decaying cities. The "last, great war" has been predicted by a number of others—dating back several centuries in some cases.

In short, catastrophic earthquakes, tornadoes, flood, famine, pestilence, war, alien invasions, and many other variations of cataclysms have been suggested by one person or another.

So what is a reasonably rational, but sensibly cautious, individual supposed to do in looking ahead to the 21st century?

The projections in this article will be based on data from several sources:

- scientific forecasting in regard to weather patterns, global warming, and similar issues
- studies of risk management by the insurance industry
- books and articles examining millennial trends in the past and present
- interpretations of the cycles of the planets (astrology)

Major Cataclysms

Meteor Massacre

Some scientists are concerned about an **asteroid or major meteor strike** to the Earth. There is more and more agreement that the extinction of the dinosaurs was probably caused by a major meteor hit off the coast of what is now Mexico. Recent evidence suggests a major meteorite hit in Nevada (at a time long ago when an ocean covered that part of the world) and many more impact craters are suspected elsewhere.

A number of astronomers have suggested we should be observing our celestial surroundings more carefully in order to prepare for any possible collisions. With enough warning, we might be able to create some kind of "Star Wars" defense or take steps to nudge aside a meteor headed on collision course with the Earth. Still, even the cautious scientists agree that while the odds of such an event are high in terms of the age of the universe, they are low in terms of any particular lifetime. Astrologically and in terms of common sense, the "terror from the skies" scenario seems improbable. It is not even on the scale yet as far as insurance companies (experts in risk management) are concerned.

A Flipped Earth

Although archaeologists can cite prior magnetic reversals of the Earth's poles, they have not engendered major catastrophes. Some of the individuals who are speaking of a "polar shift" are confusing the reversal of magnetic poles (which has happened before and does not affect climate or geography) with the actual shifting of the Earth's axis. A radical, instant **axis shift** (20 to 180 degrees suggested in various "new age" apocalyptic writings) is more than highly unlikely. It defies the laws of physics and has no support from either astrology or people in the insurance industry (who are most motivated to identify potential risks in order to protect their bottom line). It is yet another of the very common "end of the world" scenarios which tend to rise in millennial times.

If the reversal of our magnetic poles were to occur now, the ramifications would be more serious than in ancient times.

Because our modern society is so dependent upon technology, we might be somewhat at risk. Such a reversal, if instantaneous, might cause a number of airplane crashes, for example, as directional systems go haywire. Many of our tools and resources involve electromagnetic interactions, and thus could be affected. If much of modern technology were *kaput* for a time, it could be rather devastating for the people involved. Even this scenario, however, is unlikely in any near future.

A recent report noted that the Earth's magnetic field has diminished by 15% since 1600. If it continues at the present rate, it might be all gone in about 2000 more years. That could, possibly, be the beginning of a reversal of Earth's magnetic poles. Such a shift would probably take a number of years and is extremely unlikely in even the next few hundred years.

Armageddon

The history of Armageddon prophecies is quite rich. The tradition of an "end of the world" goes back to *Biblical* sources. A Christian millennium is said to last one thousand years and end with a final battle and Last Judgment of all the dead. Satan will then be bound for one thousand years while Christ returns and rules with resurrected Christian martyrs. Then, Satan will be loosed for one final battle, which is won by Jesus and his allies. At that point Satan and his ilk are cast into a "lake of fire and brimstone." All of the dead are then resurrected to either live with Jesus or end up in hell.

Jesus and his early followers expected the apocalypse to occur rather quickly—within the lifetimes of some of Jesus' followers. Around 156 AD, a man named Montanus would fall into trances and announce the Christ was about to come again. A number of people left their towns to flock to where the "New Jerusalem" was to be established. Before the turning of the year 1000, there was millennium fever. People were expecting the destruction of old ways and were less willing to be obedient and follow traditional structures.

Individuals participating in hopeless revolts were often motivated by millennium fever. (If you believe you are living at the "end of an age," you are willing to risk much!) The Anabaptist Thomas Muntzer believed this and in 1525 led the Thuringian peasants in a revolt that led to tens of thousands being killed. In the U.S., a Labadist colony was founded (around the Maryland/ Pennsylvania/ Delaware borders) in 1683. Based on the teachings of Jean de Labadie, the Labadists were trying to purify themselves for the coming millennium. Because they believed history was coming to a close, they were celibate. When the world did not end, they disbanded after about 10 years. In 1694, followers of Jacob Zimmerman (in Germantown, Pennsylvania) were expecting the millennium to arrive that year. They had an observatory on the roof of their tabernacle and expected signs in the sky to help foretell the millennium. Jacob Zimmerman himself died the day the group departed for America—an ironic note. (Perhaps he psychically foresaw his own death and confused it with the idea of the end of the world!) Zimmerman's successor suggested another date after the original date set by Zimmerman occurred and nothing happened, but adherents became disenchanted and started to fall away.

The Shakers were active in America in the 1790's. Another name for the Shakers was the United Society of Believers in Christ's Second Appearing. They were very hardworking people who were celibate and created a Millennial Church. They eventually died off.

In the early 1800's, the Rappites settled in Pennsylvania. They were another German separatist sect who practiced self-denial and celibacy in order to prepare for the millennium. Founded by George Rapp (who split from the Lutheran Church), the group fell into decline after Rapp's death in 1847.

Joseph Smith founded the Church of Jesus Christ of Latter-day Saints (called Mormons today) in 1830. Part of the basic preaching of Smith was the idea of people needing salvation in the latter days before Christ's second coming.

Perhaps as many as 100,000 people believed a William Miller (a Vermont farmer and an officer in the War of 1812) who preached of a coming apocalypse. His warnings were given support by the economic crises of the 1830's. Miller predicted that Christ would return between March 21, 1843 and March 21, 1844—and much of the world would be burned. Later, the date was set back to October 22, 1844. After the second coming did not occur, Miller's followers declined, but he and some of the remaining faithful took the name of Advent Christians. Other Advent movements occurred. Eventually, the Seventh Day Adventist Church developed.

Currently, groups such as Joehovah's Witnesses expect Christ's Second Coming in the near future and try to save the rest of us before that "ending time" arrives. A "new-age" variation on millennial themes was expressed by the small group of people who followed Marshal Applewhite. In March of 1997, 39 members of Heaven's Gate (a cult led by Applewhite) committed suicide. They expected to ascend to a higher level and hitch a ride on Comet Hale-Bopp. The group left apocalyptic messages on their Web site.

Millennium motifs have also influenced events outside the U.S. and Europe. Several failed revolts in Africa are connected to assumptions that "the end is near." Many Xhosa killed cattle and stopped cultivating because they were expecting to be reborn with wonderful, healthier cattle and to see the Europeans driven back into the sea. Similar themes contributed to the 1915 rebellion in Nysasaland (now Malawi). Likewise, among Native Americans, the Ghost Dance Movement (of the late 1800's) had clear millennium imagery predicting an apocalypse with the whites departing and the Indians gaining back all they had lost and even greater glory.

According to one poll, 25% of Americans believe Jesus Christ will come again to Earth within their lifetimes. Recent articles have trumpeted that "Twelve *Biblical* Scholars" predict the end of the world soon (based on various passages in the *Bible.*) Given the long history of anticipating the Second Coming, it is difficult to see why 2000 (or any time in the near future) should be any more likely for the apocalypse than any of the previous dates which have failed.

A Hot House Earth

Global warming (as a result of the trapping of Earth's heat by the emission of carbon dioxide and other "greenhouse gases"—mostly due to factories, automobiles and industrial development) has been a contentious issue among scientists for some time now. Although the data seem to clearly denote a trend, not everyone is convinced. Most scientists whose specialties involve the atmosphere and climatology feel the trends are clear. A U.N. report in 1995, produced with 2000 scientists from around the world, concluded that: "the balance of evidence suggests a discernible human impact on Earth's climate system." [San Diego *Union Tribune*, Tuesday, October 7, 1997, A-15]

Eskimo hunters are complaining that the ice is breaking up earlier and earlier in the season—which interferes with their hunting of walrus. Several island nations are already losing bits of land to the tide. The Maldives (an island chain in the Indian Ocean) would lose eighty percent of their land if the ocean rises only 20 inches. According to Australian researchers, the sea level has risen 1.4 inches in 25 years. A U.N. scientific panel has predicted that sea levels worldwide will rise up to 3 feet in the next century thanks to global warming. In addition to the warming, ocean currents are likely to be affected and more storms could be generated—battering fragile coastlines even more.

The U.N. scientific panel predicts—if emissions remain at current rates—that by 2100, the world's average temperature will be 2 to 6 degrees (Fahrenheit) higher and sea levels will rise by 6 inches to 3 feet. The results are also likely to contribute to more turbulent weather. Climate zones could shift hundreds of miles. Some areas will become wetter, some warmer, some colder, some drier. Human adjustments would be challenging.

Pluses could occur in some areas: e.g., new rains assisting agriculture, but minuses are also likely. New areas could be subject to mosquitoes carrying malaria or other tropical diseases. Or, if permafrost in the north softens, the foundations of buildings could be affected and roads might buckle. Glaciers would melt (contributing to rising sea levels); some animal and plant species would be killed and massive crop failures are possible with weather shifts. America could, conceivably, lose 9000 square miles of coastline.

Some of the scientists arguing against global warming have strong ties to the oil, utilities, and other industries with a vested interest in continuing to discharge hydrocarbons in large amounts. Lately, they have stropped trying to argue so much against the idea that global warming is happening and are shifting their focus to potential economic impact. They are claiming that the U.S. cannot "afford" to take the step to lessen our energy (and other) consumption which contributes to global warming. In contrast, in 1997, 2500 economists (including eight Nobel Laureates) signed a statement declaring: "Sound economic analysis shows there are policy options that would slow climate change without harming American living standards, and that these measures may in fact improve U.S. productivity in the longer run." [*The Nation*; "White House vs. Greenhouse." by David Corn, October 13, 1997, page 20] A recent newspaper editorial pointed out that industry has historically complained about the costs of various environmental protection laws (before they were passed) and that—consistently—American ingenuity and know-how has come up with new inventions and different procedures which made the environmental protection possible at a fraction of the expected costs.

Insurance companies have begun to invest in learning about global warming. When the "bean counters" at major insurance companies start to take seriously such a prospect, it is probably time to pay attention.

Individual people can take steps to protect themselves here as well. Island nations are at risk and may have to pay heavy prices to protect their lands from being overwhelmed. Some delaying measures are possible presently. (The Japanese helped to build a concrete barrier on Male island—capital of the Maldives, to protect it from high waves. But that nation cannot afford to protect all of its 200 islands at a cost of $4700 per block!) The underlying causes must be addressed.

Regardless of the laws passed by governments, each of us can lessen our own use of coal, oil, and hydrocarbons. This can be done by walking, bicycling, or using public transportation more often and a personal car less often. It can be done by supporting solar power and other forms of energy generation in which emissions are not a problem. It can be aided by planting more trees and being active to protect forests on the Earth. It can be done by choosing products with minimal packaging (especially plastics which use hydrocarbons) and recycling.

For those of us living on or near a coastline, extra motivation is present. Although sea levels are unlikely to rise sufficiently in America in our lifetime to be a problem, they could certainly affect any property we pass on to children, grandchildren, nieces, nephews, etc. If we want to alter the future, taking certain steps now is highly advisable.

Astrological patterns, although subject to interpretation, would certainly fit a hotter, dryer planet, although major shifts are still unlikely. A gradual, continued climb seems probable. Perhaps related is the issue of **water**. With many of the outer planets occupying signs associated with wind and dryness, it is likely that clean water will become much more of a problem in the near future. Between pollution, over development, dams, and over population, we are using up many of our water resources in too many parts of the world. Our underground water is being consumed at a level where replenishment is not possible. So, desalinization and even wild ideas such as towing icebergs south and melting them may become less improbable as years go by.

Good-bye California

There is no known geological or geophysical phenomenon that would cause **California to sink beneath the ocean**. This particular prediction has received support from some interpretations of the work of deceased psychic Edgar Cayce. However, current scientific evidence makes such an event unlikely. Nor are there astrological patterns to suggest California alone will perish.

There is a low-level probability that the Ross Ice Sheet will shift and bring major disaster to all coastal areas of the world, but that would not be limited to California or the western coast of the United States.

Scientists are aware that if the **Ross Ice Shelf** were to shift, it could end up in the Antarctic Sea. As a consequence, water levels would rise about twenty to one hundred feet worldwide. The result would be flooding of up to 20 miles from the sea. Most coastal towns would be inundated. The human and economic consequences would be staggering:

Certain countries, such as Bangladesh, would disappear.

Because this catastrophe would occur gradually, over a period of months, refugees from coastal areas would become a huge burden on the interior parts of every country.

Sextillions of dollars of real estate, homes, factories, and industries would be destroyed.

Many countries with sizable investment (people, business, etc.) in their coastal areas would find recovery almost impossible.

Fortunately, the likelihood of the Ross Ice Shelf shifting is extremely small.

Weather Extremes

An **increase in dangerous weather**, e.g., more hurricanes, tornadoes, earthquakes, floods, etc., appears to already be underway. Insurance companies are aware that they paid out more for damage from hurricanes, floods, etc., in the late 1980's and the first half of the 1990's than they had paid in the previous three decades! The economic price of "natural disasters" has tripled. Damages were $40 billion in the 1960's and were $120 billion in the 1980's. In the United States alone, four disasters since 1989 have each cost more than one billion dollars in Federal Emergency Management Agency (FEMA) funds. Scientists agree that weather runs in cycles and some suspect that we are headed for a more unstable period.

An astrological pattern which supports this weather change has to do with the solar system barycenter. The barycenter is the center of mass in our solar system and it can move from close to the center of the sun to as far out as one solar radius beyond the sun's surface. Normally the orbit of everything in the solar system around the sun's barycenter is counter-clockwise. Occasionally, however, the Sun moves clockwise with respect to the barycenter. This has happened seven times in the last 3400 years.

The clockwise movement occurred in 1632-1633, in 1810-1812 and in 1989-1990. The first two periods were followed historically by unseasonable and extreme weather. In the 1630's and 1640's, the River Thames froze solidly and people had "frost fairs" on the ice of the river. There were short growing seasons and the American colonies had one of the three worst winters of that century in 1641. Concentrations of volcanic activity were the most intense of the previous 500 years.

Weather following the 1810-1812 period was also quite extreme. In 1816, we had the "year without a summer" when the eastern U.S. and Europe had freezing weather every single month of the year. The combination of short growing seasons and cold summers led to famine in places such as the Ukraine and Switzerland. One historian noted the period was also followed by political upheavals, pandemics, lots of migration, and economic upheaval.

We've already seen considerable political upheaval for the current period (the two to three decades following the clockwise cycle for the barycenter): the fall of the Berlin Wall, problems in the former Yugoslavia, the break-up of the Soviet Union and emergence of new, independent states, and the struggles in Rwanda and other parts of Africa. It seems logical to conclude that we are likely to have to continue to face considerable disruption both in weather and politics for another 15 to 20 years.

Although the overall pattern applies to the whole Earth, that does not mean that individuals are helpless. There is much that each of us can do. If hurricanes are common in your area, get hurricane straps for the roof of your house. Purchase storm shutters for your windows. If you have settled in a flood plain, strongly consider relocating! If you must stay in an area which is high risk for flooding, make sure you get insurance. In earthquake-prone California, we can all make sure that our water heaters are strapped to the wall. (Fires are a major problem after many earthquakes.)

Both businesses and families ought to have plans for emergencies. How will you continue to live and work if faced with a natural disaster? One simple precaution is to be sure that you have the water, stored food, supplies and tools to be able to survive at least three days if you ended up cut off from the world due to one catastrophe or another. Being prepared and reducing our personal risks improves our own chances even though the odds of bad weather for the world in general are rising.

Disease

The issue of new and deadly pestilences spreading rapidly throughout the world is a real one to some extent. Scientists point to certain tropical diseases which are spreading to parts of the world never before afflicted (probably due to global warming). The era of mass transportation has meant that disease carriers (insects, food, people, etc.) can easily and quickly be moved from one territory to another. In cases of highly contagious diseases, the danger is extremely great. This is why people have been so cautious about the Ebola Virus (dramatized and fictionalized by Hollywood in the movie *Outbreak*).

The fact is, we truly are one world in terms of health concerns, but people have not yet woken up to that fact. Regardless of spiritual principles, it would behoove people in the countries with a higher standard of living to aid health efforts in poorer countries. Neglecting disease in any part of the globe puts us all at risk. One of the major medical threats now is certain bacteria which are now totally resistant to *any* of our current medications. These resistant strains have developed partially due to overuse of antibiotics and other tools (which were considered almost magical when they first came out and medical professionals did not realize that they could become ineffective). However, another major factor is individuals who stop taking their medication as soon as they feel better, but before the invading organisms have been fully killed. (This is more likely to happen in poor countries because medication is expensive.) Those invading organisms then have the opportunity to mutate and some have mutated into forms against which *all* of our current medications are useless. We can expect more of this in the future.

What can we do as individuals about this threat? We can take several steps:

Be cautious about where we travel and what we expose ourselves to.

Become active in educating the medical profession and ordinary people about the overuse of antibiotics.

Support medical research for new "magic bullets."

Give generously to organizations which help to promote health everywhere in the world.

Watch the latest research in terms of vitamins, exercises, and other techniques to strengthen our immune systems and make us less susceptible to disease.

Outside Forces

Little Green (or Gray) Men

One of the more popular disaster scenarios (amply illustrated by Hollywood in a few recent blockbusters) is the theme of **alien invasion**. Although the odds makers in Las Vegas have, in recent years, lowered the odds for this occurrence, the chances are still rated pretty darn high that we won't be meeting aliens soon! Suspicions in regard to U.F.O.'s (unidentified flying objects) go far back. Although Roswell, New Mexico received much coverage recently (having celebrated its 50th anniversary of "The Incident"), some people concerned with the question of extraterrestrial contact point to the *Bible* as containing an early reference to a U.F.O. (Remember the song: "Ezekiel saw a wheel, way up in the middle of the sky.") Although a number of people believe they have seen U.F.O.'s and even been abducted by aliens, there is no credible evidence for any widespread invasion. Even if one accepts many of the assumptions of people who feel they have "made contact," their stories relate more to scientific investigation or medical experimentation. Few are suggesting that our civilization is about to be overrun by aliens. Meanwhile, project SETI (the search by scientists for intelligent extraterrestrial life) continues to bomb out. Science fiction as literature and movies is apt to continue to be popular, but as a mirror to life—extremely unlikely—at least for the near future.

Sociological Factors

Splinter Groups

With the break-up of the Soviet Union and many of the trials and tribulations in Africa, we appear to be in an era of increased **tribalism**. People are identifying with smaller groups rather than larger ones. In some cases, the associated "ethnic cleansing" is horrifying. We've seen people kill people who have been their friends and neighbors for years "because" they belonged to a slightly different ethnic group or followed a different religion. Unfortunately, some of the astrological patterns discussed below (including Pluto transiting the sign of Sagittarius) suggest this will continue to be a trend into the 21st century.

"Holy" Wars

The outlook in terms of **religious fanaticism** is rather depressing. We have seen a rise in fundamentalism on a number of fronts and that often correlates with increased violence. When a religious group is convinced that its beliefs are the only "real" truth, all too often the "next" step is to kill people who do not share those beliefs. The perpetrators of the Inquisition believed they were saving souls. The people who murder in the name of a loving God have convinced themselves that the Almighty is on their side. Again, the astrological patterns suggest that this trend will continue for at least another 10 years.

As individuals, what are our options? We can practice tolerance and offer a constructive example. (Never underestimate the power of a good example!) We can offer educational materials. People who are fully aware of the incredible, infinite vastness of the universe will sometimes begin to question the idea of an intensely personal God who is obsessed with practices upon Earth. Some people will outgrow a narrow view of religion through exposure to other cultures and other ideas. We can also be eternally vigilant (the price of liberty, as Jefferson wrote) about fascistic movements, even cloaked in religion. Holocausts happen more easily when good people choose to look away. We can remain active and involved in the political process as well as promoting good in our own lives and communities.

Financial Disasters

One of the economically oriented scenarios making the rounds in our millennium times is the idea of a coming **worldwide depression**. This is sometimes linked to a major Stock Market collapse. Financial analysts have long known that people react more to "outright" paper losses than to "missed opportunities." (That is, an individual is more upset when s/he buys a stock which proceeds to go down 10 points than when s/he loses out on a chance to buy a stock which goes up 10 points.) So, the "doom-and-gloomers" have a built-in audience. (Plus, marketing researchers have long known that fear is a major motivator for people.)

The classic "millennium fever" of "ending times" just before the close of a thousand-year period feeds disaster scenarios. So, the Stock Market bears can play right into people's concerns about the turn of this century. Various conspiracy theories also abound which ascribe the predicted financial collapse to a nefarious cabal (of whatever ethnic or religious group is preferred for scapegoating), the political errors of the U.S. (blamed on either the right or the left depending on who is writing the script for the catastrophe), human greed which requires God to wipe the Earth clean and start again, etc.

Ironically, around the anniversary of the 1987 Stock Market Crash (in the U.S.), we saw Hong Kong's Stock Market approach melt-down with consequences reverberating through all the markets worldwide. Need we doubt any longer that we are part of a truly global economy? The "oneness" that is a goal of many spiritual groups already exists on important levels, but we humans have yet to understand all the ramifications involved!

Although a worldwide depression is possible, we know that the powers-that-be (movers and shakers economically and politically) will do everything possible to avoid it because—frankly—it is bad for business and their power goals. Given the current astrological cycles, it does not seem likely. We are in a continuing struggle over the balance between the "haves" and the "have nots"—inside the U.S. as well as in the world. The gaps between rich and poor are getting wider rather than shrinking. The salary differential between an average worker in the U.S. and the CEO of a company is incredibly high—and much greater than in other "developed" nations (e.g., Japan, western Europe, etc.). It is likely that this trend of larger gaps will continue for a time yet. If it gets too great, then revolutionary potentials will arise once more. For the near future, however, it seems likely that current economic practices will continue.

We will have a crisis with the year 2000—having to do with our computer systems (which have not been updated so that the year 2000 will register in computer code as 2000 rather than 1900). Current estimates are that many essential programs will not be updated by January 1, 2000. The consequences of this could range from a great deal of annoyance to major snafus if important banking, government, transportation, or other services are not ready for the new century! This exigency, however, is not due to any particular "magic" about the year 2000, but due to human lack of foresight. The likelihood is that considerable annoyance and some disruption will occur, but we will muddle through overall. Considerable economic toll (lost productivity) is possible, but it is unlikely to be enough to trigger a depression.

A Golden Age

The rosy scenario which is making the rounds, particularly in some new-age circles, is that we are at the dawn of a new age, that the "peace, harmony and understanding" promised in the song "The Age of Aquarius" are just around the corner. This radical shift is variously ascribed to a change in humanity's consciousness, the intervention of angels or other celestial or extraterrestrial beings, the meditative powers of a key group of highly evolved people, etc.

If we examine history, the likelihood of that sort of intervention seems very small. If we look at psychology, the possibility of such a shift in consciousness is less than miniscule. Or, as my teacher used to say: "We'll get a golden age when we get golden people." Humans are fallible and far from perfect.

The Born Again equivalent of this scenario is the Second Coming of Jesus Christ. According to polls, about one-fourth of Americans believe that Jesus will return within their lifetimes. Faith can certainly move mountains and cure some ailments, but skepticism reigns in regard to this event. The odds makers would probably not even consider it.

World War III

Various new-age sources (mentioned earlier) have predicted the coming of World War III, usually associated with small wars in the Middle East getting out of hand. With the break-up of the former Soviet Union, a nuclear armageddon has become less likely. Although individual terrorist groups and nations will, unfortunately, have some access to nuclear weapons and more to biological threats, the likelihood of a worldwide holocaust is actually rather small at this point. Humanity does appear to have reached a critical level of consciousness in stepping back from the brink of a war of total destruction. The leaders we are currently selecting have no desire for mass suicide.

Astrological Cycles

So what insights does astrology have to offer in regard to these various possibilities?

One of the major astrological cycles is made up of the entry of the planets into each sign of zodiac. The year 2000 is not a pivotal one in terms of sign changes. Uranus will be more than halfway through its sojourn in Aquarius. Neptune will have entered Aquarius in 1998 and Pluto will be about one-third of its way through Sagittarius. Jupiter and Saturn will both enter the sign of Gemini—but not at the "dawning" of the "new millennium." Jupiter enters Gemini in July and Saturn in August. Since Jupiter changes sign about once a year and Saturn about every 2-1/2 years, these movements are not highly significant.

The lack of major cycle changes in the year 2000 is one of the reasons most astrologers give little weight to that particular year. As Zip Dobyns discusses in her article, 2000 has been played up in the media although there is little support for highlighting it in terms of calendars and astrological cycles. Indeed, scientists will also tell you that 2001 is the proper "new beginning" for the next century—not 2000. But that will not stop many people from partying and attributing major significance to the time our calendars roll over to a two followed by three zeros!

Another major cycle is the conjunction of two outer planets. We had several major conjunctions in the late 1980's and early 1990's. Uranus and Neptune conjuncted in Capricorn in 1993. (The previous conjunction was in 1821.) Saturn and Uranus conjuncted in 1988. (The previous conjunction was 1942—during World War II.) Saturn and Neptune conjuncted in 1989. Astrologers had noted that conjunction correlates with developments of Communism on Earth. The conjunction of 1846 marks the development and spread of communist theories. The Saturn/Neptune conjunction in 1917 marked the Russian Revolution. The next conjunction in 1952/53 marked the death of Stalin and changes in the Soviet Union. The following conjunction, in 1989, saw the fall of the Berlin Wall and reunification of Germany. The next Saturn/Neptune conjunction occurs in 2026—a time likely to mark the final end of Communism—or a radical transformation.

A cycle which is quite familiar in timing to many Americans is the Jupiter Saturn conjunction which occurs approximately every 20 years. Many Americans are aware of the "jinx" on the U.S. Presidency related to this cycle. Presidents elected in years ending in zero have died in office. Jupiter and Saturn joined one another in an earth sign from 1842 through 1961. The following Presidents all died in office: Harrison (elected in 1840), Lincoln (1860), Garfield (1880), McKinley (1900), Harding (1920), Roosevelt (1940) and Kennedy (1960).

Reagan (elected 1980) escaped this pattern, although he was the victim of an attempted assassination and probably would have died if not for modern medicine. The Jupiter/Saturn conjunction of that period was in an air sign (as opposed to an earth sign), so perhaps the cycle was broken. However, Jupiter and Saturn conjunct once more—in an earth sign—in 2000, leading many astrologers to suspect that the President elected in that year will be at risk.

So, much of what we are dealing with in 2000 and beyond, in astrological terms, is a continuation of cycles which will have begun earlier. Here is a preview of what astrology would suggest in regard to these cycles.

Sign Changes of the Outer Planets

Uranus in Aquarius: 1995-2003

The last time Uranus was in Aquarius, from 1912 to 1920, we made income tax into law. That led several astrologers to suggest that this cycle would see major revisions in our tax laws or the Internal Revenue Services. Such developments are beginning to look more likely at this time! The IRS has been subject to hearings regarding its abuses and Congress is exploring different ideas for improvement. Woodrow Wilson, a former professor and president of Princeton University, was elected President in the early part of our century (Aquarius is associated with the intellect). Bill Clinton, a Rhodes scholar, was reelected during this second cycle. We also had our first World War during Uranus' last sojourn. Uranus and Aquarius, in their worst expression, can denote a cold, uncaring, inhuman detachment. Abstract principles may be given more significance than people.

Although we can expect to escape the horrors of another world war, the detachment potential of Uranus in Aquarius is considerable. We can expect continued horrors to be perpetrated in the name of "principle" (including nationalism, ethnic cleansing, tribalism or other belief systems which are willing to kill human beings to protect an abstract position).

Neptune in Aquarius: 1998-2012

The last time Neptune was in Aquarius was from 1834-1848. During that period, the Morse Code and first electric telegraph were invented as well as the laws of thermodynamics. We had the Alamo, the Mexican War, the potato famine in Ireland, and Livingston's explorations of Africa. In China, the Opium Wars occurred. Failed revolutionary ideals in Germany brought German immigrants to the U.S. in large numbers.

During our current period, we can expect that famine will be a problem for some parts of the world—not so much because of weather (although part of the blame will fall there), but because of continuing lack of equitable distribution of what food is produced on Earth. We would expect some significant technological breakthroughs (such as the copper computer chip recently announced by IBM). Increased communication (parallel to the telegraph) is likely and the telecommunications industries of the world, along with the Internet, seem poised for it. Drugs are likely to be an ongoing focus for the next 15 years (reflecting the connection to opium from the earlier period). Challenges in regard to the mass transportation of disease carriers and the development of drug-resistant strains of bacteria are likely to continue.

Pluto in Sagittarius: 1995-2009

The last time Pluto was in Sagittarius was from 1749 to 1762. This marked the beginning of the Industrial Revolution and of the British empire in India. Benjamin Franklin flew his famous kite and invented the lightning rod and the first encyclopedia was published. Exploration and settlement of the New World by Europeans continued. Following the disillusionment of all the killing of the Inquisition, people had turned toward "The Age of Reason" and somewhat away from religion. This period in the 1700's saw an intense reform movement in England (led by John Wesley) which became Methodism. In the U.S., the "Great Revival" took place. Fundamentalists held tent meetings for the first time (the roots of our "born again" population).

This time around, we can expect our exploring and settlement to venture into outer space (the space station, for example) and inner space. Masses of information (including encyclopedias and references of all sorts) are now widely available online. Cyberspace is proving to be a significant new frontier for many of us. Economists and historians are speaking of the Information Revolution which is replacing the Industrial Revolution (and leading too many of us into lives as couch potatoes with consequent disadvantages to our health). We would expect the future to hold more religious fundamentalism and fanaticism. The fierce emotions symbolized by Pluto can lead to excessive fervor in regard to the beliefs systems, philosophies, and religions represented by Sagittarius.

A Look at the Horoscopes for 2000 and 2001

Even though the years 2000 and 2001 are artificial in terms of any major cycles, they are the "turning points" highlighted by our calendar and the media. So, it could be instructive to examine horoscopes for that time. The chart in the appendix was run for January 1, 2000, for Washington, D.C. (the center of American government).

Guessing details from charts is always a tantalizing exercise. Each planet means many different things, even in mundane (world event) astrology. So, which meaning do we assign in each particular case? The following are highly speculative possibilities for the future. Associated with each projection are the astrological placements which led to that conclusion.

Chart for Year 2000

With a strong Ceres/Ascendant contact, we would suspect that the issue of unions and employees would become more central. Concerns about grain (Ceres rules cereal) are also possible. We may get pulled into famines elsewhere as we continue to try to be the breadbasket to the world. Issues around daycare, the working mother (on or off welfare), and overpopulation are likely to continue. (Ceres represents the Earth Mother function.) As a nation, we cannot make up our mind: we want wealthy women to stay home and take care of the kids, but we want welfare mother to go out and work. That issue is likely to continue to cause controversy in 2000. (The conjunction of the Moon to the Ascendant/Chiron midpoint backs up overly idealistic expectations of how women are "supposed" to act.) Perhaps we will finally act more on the connection between feeding everyone and controlling our fertility.

Continued stock market concerns about a likely "correction" can be expected with the Moon and Saturn opposite each other across the financial houses. The Moon also squares the Uranus/Neptune midpoint (instability, confusion). It appears, however, that the rich will continue to get richer with Saturn trine the Sun and the Moon sextile the Sun.

People will continue to feel more and more torn between home/family and career demands on time and energy (another meaning of the Moon/Saturn opposition). There might also be a literal separation between whoever represents Mother (Moon) to our nation and the person who represents Father (Saturn). [Pessimistically, this could relate to the Saturn/Jupiter cycle which recurs in 2000 and may threaten the President of that time.]

Old troubles about religion are likely to surface with Neptune conjuncting the South Node of the Moon. The Mid-East is a likely place, but other regions would be possible as well. In general, religious fanaticism (indicated in another form with the Pluto/Chiron conjunction) might reach a point where the powers-that-be feel they must take action. (Pluto and Chiron quincunx Saturn with Saturn representing the Establishment and quincunxes often indicating a separation, new direction, fork in the road, or loss).

Intellectual breakthroughs are likely to continue to be profitable with Mercury semi-sextile Venus and widely trine Jupiter. Even if Congress passes the law under consideration to give corporations more power over inventions, it seems likely traditional American ingenuity will still manage. Jupiter's conjunction to midpoint of the Midheaven (power, status, contribution to society) and Uranus (inventiveness, originality) repeats the theme. Since Mercury conjuncts the Venus/Neptune midpoint, mental agility (Mercury) could be tied to resources and pleasure (Venus) through beauty or imagination (Neptune). Less constructively, the thinking (Mercury) of the populace could be focused on sensual gratification and escapism (Venus/Neptune).

Anti-government rhetoric and popular mythology will probably continue (Asc square MC) trying to present the rugged individual as the hero and government regulations as the villain.

Chart for 2001

Women are likely to have to deal with more unrealistic imagery (with Moon/Neptune semi-square). The old dichotomies of Madonna/Whore may receive new play and attention. Religion (Neptune) will probably play an important role in the visions (about women—Moon) which are promoted. Scandals could develop in regard to a mother figure, motherhood, childcare, real estate, or food. (Cutbacks at the FDA may lead to unpleasant consequences.) Some of the drawbacks of "cocooning" (withdrawing more and more into the home) are likely to emerge.

Since the Moon and Neptune are both water planets, the issue of clean (and available!) water is likely to become of more concern in 2001.

Muckracking journalism may pick up with Mercury semi-sextile Pluto. Secrets could be uncovered. Some of the scandals possible with Moon/Neptune could be aired by the press. Power (Pluto) is connected to media so entities such as Microsoft may increase their attempts to gain monopolies, even within businesses involving news and information.

Old issues about education are likely to be replayed (with Mercury conjuncting the South Node of the Moon). We can expect more talk of changing public schools. The call for "back to the basics" is likely to be stronger with Mercury's placement in the conservative sign of Capricorn and the 4th house which relates to ancestors and tradition.

With Venus conjunct Vesta, working partnerships are emphasized for the U.S., but the probability exists of some tension and critical judgments. The square to Saturn reiterates the likelihood of some clashes in our relationships with other countries—especially those seen as partners or allies. We can guess that Japan is probably one of these—more trade wars perhaps?

Neptune, associated with idealism, scandals and drugs, is closely square Mars (a key to men, sports, the military and sexual drive). Can we expect another wave of dillusionment about drugs in professional sports or in the military? Will sexual harrassment issues continue to be in the headlines? Will attempts be made to glorify war or military force (another "good" little war)? Certainly all of the above are possible.

SUMMARY

Oneness is really already here—people just don't realize it. The interconnectedness of life is very clear, but we are seeing it on a physical, mental, and cultural level and are far, far from achieving it on a spiritual level.

The cosmos has quite an ironic sense of humor. Many spiritual and environmental organizations have been promoting the idea of one Earth, trying to get people to truly empathize with the pain and suffering of others, to work to make a difference. While emotional and spiritual growth has been frustratingly slow, the physical ties have progressed very rapidly.

In terms of telecommunications, the world is one. (With the advent of the Internet and faxes, even events such as Tienaman Square in China cannot be hidden from the rest of the world. Too many channels of communication exist for any part of the globe to be totally cut off.)

In regard to disease and health issues, we are all in this together. A danger in one part of the world can all too quickly become a threat to every one of us.

In terms of environmental impact, we are interconnected. The garbage spewed out by humans has been found in the ices of Antarctica (and even on the Moon). As much as we may try to hide our heads in the sands, we are all impacting this planet—and not for the best in many ways! The cliché about the movement of a butterfly's wings in Brazil triggering a hurricane off the Mexican Coast is not a fantasy.

In terms of economic interdependency, we are just beginning to realize what a "global economy" truly means.

Despite human tendencies toward separation and scapegoating of "the other" (witness the rise of tribalism and religious wars), we live in a time when we are being forced to see how very much tied together the world is. It is as if the Cosmic Power that lies behind everything set this up so that we would **have** to learn how to love one another, to tune into each other's needs (or we'll die, taking the Earth with us.) We may end up evolving spiritually because the physical consequences of anything else are simply too severe.

It will be a highly ironic scenario if spiritual Oneness becomes possible because of the material Oneness and interconnected world we have created.

Isolationism is no longer possible. Each of us has the choice, in the coming millennium, to promote more spiritual understanding, more acceptance of the bonds that link all human beings, more education about the subtle interdependencies that connect us all—or to avoid the trend which is so apparent and contribute to the destruction of the Earth and all upon it.

Our choices, our attitudes, and our actions are what will write future history. The trends are clear. Each of us chooses, every day, with a myriad of small decisions, to what degree we support Oneness. Each of us is that symbolic drop of water in a large ocean. As each drop of water contributes to the whole, so will the ocean be purified or poisoned.

May each of us find the path which brings personal satisfaction and contributes to universal well-being.

MILLENNIAL FEVER

Millennial fever is building. The conspiracy theories are prolif-
erating, along with the prophecies that the end of the world is
imminent, or at least doom and gloom is coming to unbelievers.
The stories are coming from many sources, ranging from the
"alternative" (as opposed to mainline) media, to fundamentalist religious leaders in many groups including native peoples,
to self-proclaimed gurus of Wall St., to men in jail (or hiding)
who accuse government officials, especially U.S. intelligence
agencies, of crimes. Some of the deluge is probably
disinformation. Divide and conquer is still a popular way to
stay in power. Some of it is defensive or just self-serving.
Some of it is fantasy. Some of it is a too literal interpretation of
symbolic myths.

In the explosive deluge of information, there seem to be
three main sources of the "truly" millennial type of material.
The bulk of the conspiracy theories emphasize some variety of
political and/or economic disaster. They appear to be exag-
gerations of some underlying facts that are being offered to the
public for a variety of reasons. The most obvious one is that
books, magazines, and newspapers make money from them, for
the authors and the publishers. They help Wall Street gurus
sell their high-priced newsletters. People in jail or hiding from
authorities claim they were only taking orders and their bosses
are the real criminals. Militias gain converts, adding to their

ranks. With all belief systems, the larger the group, the more its proselytizers are reassured that their beliefs are true. When the group is really revolutionary, they have an extra need for the sense of safety associated with numbers. In addition to whatever profit is gained by the conspiracy promoters, their claims add to the millennial fever in the atmosphere. Though not all can be called "truly millennial," they are adding fuel to the fire.

My primary goal in this book is to compare a panoramic sweep of archaeology and history against the actual dates of the astrological ages, examining possible matches between the shifting position of the sun at the vernal equinox as it has moved in front of the constellations and the times of major changes in the lives of evolving humans. But before I discuss the astronomy and archaeology, I want to survey the current millennial scene material, pointing out some of its sources and trying to sort out what I see as major confusion in much of the material coming from ostensibly "spiritual" groups, whether traditional or "new age."

One obvious thread of millennial beliefs is well-known. Norman Cohn's book *Cosmos, Chaos, and the World to Come*, is a good source for this information. The book was updated by Cohn and republished by Yale University Press in 1993. His theories are largely accepted by historians who trace the history of religion. The ancient world mostly believed in repetitive cycles. One age would end, only to be followed by a new age. If one creation was destroyed, which happened periodically, another would be produced by some variety of gods. Cohn suggests that the primary early source of the idea of a final triumph of good over evil stems from Zoroaster, a teacher in what is now Iran. Dates for his life are uncertain, but are often estimated to be about 1500 BC. This "apocalyptic" faith was especially appealing to people when they were living in very unstable and stressful times, when the present was miserable and the future seemed both unpredictable and threatening. It was especially attractive since it could "explain" the current misery without challenging the basic religious beliefs. The true believers could still have faith in both the power and the goodness of their god with the reassurance that eventually

He would overcome all chaos and evil in the world (which was conveniently blamed on an evil demiurge or lesser god) and the faithful believers would be rewarded by eternal bliss.

This apocalyptic belief was preached by a variety of Jewish prophets during times when the Hebrews were under major stress, conquered and ruled by a foreign power, or even sent into exile away from their homeland. Daniel is probably the most quoted of these prophets. Many of the early Christians accepted the idea of an "end time" when God (in the form of Jesus to the Christians) would destroy all non-believers and the faithful would inherit the earth to live forever in peace. *The Book of Revelations* is the most elaborate source of these ideas, and modern fundamentalist Christians pour over *The Bible* and watch the news, looking for the signs which will signal the day of Armageddon — the final battle of good and evil which is to take place on the plains not far from Jerusalem. For years, it was widely accepted by Protestants that the Roman Catholic Church was the Beast who would be conquered. Then, Russia was identified as the target. Since the breakup of the Soviet Union, Saddam Hussein is being nominated by some to play that role.

Over the centuries, the "great day of reckoning" has been predicted many times. True believers have gathered on hilltops in many countries, often having sold all their possessions, wearing white robes, expecting to be picked up and carried to heaven, only to be disillusioned. A doubter might wonder why they "sold" their possessions instead of just giving them away, since presumably the money was not needed in heaven or in the new paradise to come on earth. Some have taken very painful routes to attain what they believed would be their reward in heaven — witness David Koresh at Waco.

Another good book for those who want more information on recent fundamentalists is *When Time Shall Be No More* by Paul Boyer, published by Harvard University Press in 1992. Boyer writes that in gathering information for his book, he read about 100 pre-1945 books and over 200 post-1945 books on prophecy. He also read the published papers of 8 prophecy conferences between the 1870s and the 1970s, and about 25 prophecy newsletters and religious periodicals on the subject.

I did not manage the time to read his whole book, but I think that he mostly stayed with the Judaeo-Christian material.

A variety of native peoples have had their own versions of this ancient hope that their gods would come to their rescue, validate their traditional beliefs and ways, destroy their oppressors, and give them an earthly paradise. The Ghost Dance Cult of the Plains Indians in the 19th century in the U.S. promised this if the believers performed the proper, painful rituals. Their special blessed shirts were supposed to protect them from the white man's bullets, but they did not work. Some Hopi Indians in the U.S. southwest still look for the return of their "elder brother" who is to come reinforced by the traditional gods to bring honor and restitution to the Hopis. The believers say that it is only the continuing Hopi rituals which keep the earth rotating properly. In a video released in recent years, the same claim was made by a group of natives in South America. The birth of a white buffalo on August 20, 1994 on a small farm in Janesville, Wisconsin, is being heralded by some American Indians as a sign of a prophesied new spiritual age.

Earlier in this century, the Cargo Cult in Melanesia described by anthropologist Melanowski offered a variation to a people overwhelmed by western "civilization." Linda Schele and David Freidel's book *Maya Cosmos* describes the beliefs still held by Cruzob Mayas who are preoccupied by war and the imminent end of the world. They believe there will be a great war with all societies fighting each other, that the machines will be destroyed and the armies reduced to fighting with machetes and sticks. They say that their people will win because they have kept faith and listened to their "talking crosses" and a Maya King will rule the lands.

The various belief systems lumped as "new age" offer their own versions of apocalypse. For example, the August 1996 issue of *Fate Magazine* has an article from someone who obviously knows almost nothing about astrology, listing May 5, 2000 as doomsday, and blaming it on the fact that several planets will be "lined up" in Taurus. The author quotes Richard Kieninger, author of *The Ultimate Frontier*, as the original source of this prediction. Richard Noone's book *Ice: The Ulti-*

mate Disaster, agrees and thinks a polar flip is coming on that date. Astrologers know that we have had as many planets in a single sign several times already in this century without any noticeable tremor in our world. The latest version of the polar shift was passed on to me by a friend as this book was being written in the fall of 1997. My friend was not sure of the source, but suspected that it was Gordon Scallion who has been predicting 8 and 9 magnitude earthquakes in California for the last few years. The psychic channeler named the afternoon of December 27, 1997 as the time for the polar shift. Obviously, if his information had been correct, you would not be reading this book. Of course, I ran a horoscope for December 27 and saw no reason for alarm. One more recent prediction which picks a different date in 2000 for "the end," appeared in the November 18, 1997 issue of the tabloid *Weekly World News*. Marc Padger, who claims to be a former CIA agent, states that the U.S. captured a space alien on June 20. The alien is said to have learned English in a single afternoon, and to have told his CIA captors that God was so furious with His creations everywhere, He had already destroyed at least 4,000 planets and that Earth was next, scheduled to burn and explode on January 11, 2000. A chart for that day suggested the usual clash between beliefs and physical reality. The profit motive is the only reason I can see for printing such fantasy.

Some of the current true believers have accepted the ideas of native spiritual leaders. Sometimes, the faithful are to be picked up by a UFO just before the catastrophe comes to earth. The form of final catastrophe is often described as geological. Continental edges are to sink beneath the ocean which is to inundate large inland areas as well. Volcanoes and earthquakes are to create widespread destruction, and the poles are to "shift" or "flip," leading to tidal waves washing over the earth and killing most of its inhabitants. In Noone's version, an imbalance of the ice at the poles is to produce a slipping of the earth's crust like a loosely attached skin slipping and rotating part of the way around the core of a grape. Marshall Applewhite, known to his followers as Bo, led his group of 38 true believers in a mass suicide on the weekend of March 25-27, 1997 in Rancho Santa Fe, California. They announced that they were joining their friends in a spaceship which was following the Hale-Bopp comet, leaving Earth before the coming catastrophes.

Some of the "true believers" in a polar shift are confusing the Noone scenario with the reversal of earth's magnetic poles which is a genuine phenomena. An article by Robert Kunzig in the December 1997 issue of *Discover* magazine discussed the finding of ancient humans in Spain below the boundary between Lower Pleistocene and the Middle Pleistocene. This boundary is defined as the last time Earth's magnetic field switched direction, around 780,000 years ago. What had been north became south and vice versa. Gary Glatzmaier of the Institute of Geophysics & Planetary Physics at Los Alamos National Laboratory has done extensive work on magnetic pole reversals. In an Internet response to a question about the phenomena, Glatzmaier stated that the reversal process on Earth is not regular as it is on the Sun where it occurs every 11 years. On Earth, the intervals between reversals can range from about 10,00 years to as much as 25 million years, and it may take 5,000 years for the reversal to be complete. He added that we still do not know enough about the Earth's core to predict exactly when reversals will occur or how long they will take.

An alternative to the geological scenarios offered by a psychic channeler calls for intervention by the "White Brotherhood" who have reportedly decided that humans are not going to ever "get it" on their own, so the spiritual teachers plan to accelerate Karma. This is a less bloody version of the myth. The ruling elite of the earth, who are driven by their greed for power and wealth, will experience breakdowns in their immune systems and will self-destruct, leaving the earth to the loving and sharing people. This would be a major change since all of the recent studies have shown that individuals with more money and more education live longer and remain more healthy. Some "new age" and financial gurus sound rather similar, with predictions of a total breakdown of the world's economic system. For some, the ballooning debt will finally destroy the system. For others, the geological disasters will wipe out the insurance companies and the rest of the financial establishment will fall into the abyss after them. These visions were produced before the U.S. started reducing its deficit.

The San Diego, California daily newspaper, the *Union Tribune*, carried a series of articles on religious cults in early November 1997. One of the featured groups lives in Sedona, Arizona, and has many similarities to the Heaven's Gate group led by Bo. Their leader calls himself Gabriel, and according to former members, he wields total power in the group, one of the primary features which differentiates a cult from a religion. Admittedly, the boundary can be fuzzy when we consider the Roman Catholic Pope's claim to final authority over what are acceptable beliefs and behavior, and the claim by conservative Jews that orthodox and reformed Jews are not "true" Jews.

In the *Union Tribune* article, Gabriel claims to channel unseen celestial beings who agree with Kieninger's date of May 2000 as the day of destruction, though Gabriel says it might be May 2001. During the intervening time, which is just over two years from the time this book is being written, Gabriel suggests that the U.S. might be invaded by the Chinese Red Army, but he mostly sticks with the massive earth changes predicted originally by Edgar Cayce which continue to be repeated by a variety of more contemporary psychics. California is supposed to fall in the ocean along with the east coast, monster floods are expected, but also global water shortages. If Sedona proves unsafe, the Aquarian Concepts "family" will be beamed into the cosmos or evacuated from the planet by friendly spaceships. Following the big disaster, Gabriel is quoted as saying that his group will rule the earth as part of a "Divine Administration" of "Divine New Order." According to Gabriel, they will be in control of the whole planet from their center five miles outside of Sedona which they call "Planetary Headquarters."

According to the *Union Tribune* article, Gabriel was born as Tony Delevin in Pittsburgh, Pennsylvania on July 5, 1947. I do not have his time of birth, but if astrologers reading this book want to experiment with his chart, they might try putting Neptune on the Ascendant. Gabriel lists many notable past lives for himself, including Alexander the Great, the apostle Peter, and St. Francis of Assisi. When questioned about the parallels between his group and the Heaven's Gate cult, Gabriel said that their suicide was selfish. They should have stayed on earth and tried to make a difference. And he did leave himself an out on the coming destruction. He said that if the planet returned to God, the global destruction could be averted.

Needless to say, some dramatic astrological patterns would be needed for any of these "total" scenarios, so most practicing astrologers remain skeptical. I think that most astrologers see problems due to human inhumanity to fellow humans and threats to earth's ecology from over-population by humans, but not the end of the world.

Shifting to the central concern of this book, there is another primary source of these apocalyptic scenarios which is totally mixed in with the wishful thinking that the "elect" (which is naturally always our own group) will soon live happily ever after, even if a lot of other people have to die to produce this "happy ending." This important source is ancient astrology. As far as I know, the first book to present this information was *Hamlet's Mill* by Giorgio de Santillana and Hertha von Dechend, published by Gambit Inc., in 1969. It was later reprinted by Weiser in NY. A recent book which follows up that seminal work is *The Secret of the Incas* by William Sullivan, published by Crown in 1996. I have written previously about this basic theory about astrological ages in the Gemini 1984 and Gemini 1994 issues of my quarterly publication, the *Mutable Dilemma*.

We know from Marshak's work presented in *The Roots of Civilization* that humans have been using the sky as their clock and calendar for at least 20,000 years. Neolithic hunters marked the phases of the Moon on reindeer bones and horns. Though we have no irrefutable evidence, it seem very possible that by the time writing was developed, starting around 3500 BC, the ancient world recognized the equinoxes and solstices as major turning points in the year. They were like the corners of a circle, when the relative length of day and night changed. Major monuments like Stonehenge and Mayan temples and simple stone circles among preliterate people were used to identify these days, and vital rituals were performed on them.

By 8,000 BC, agriculture and domestic animals were producing enough surplus food to allow specialists in the expanding villages. The observation of the sky, both for its value as a calendar and as a religion, would bring the recognition of the "precession" of the equinoxes as, over the years, these important dates shifted against the backdrop of the star groups called constellations.

A variety of myths described this observed fact that the spring equinox which had formerly occurred when the Sun was in the constellation of Taurus was now occurring in the constellation of Aries. The worship of the Bull was replaced by the veneration of the Ram, and then by the Christian symbol of the two Fishes. To a human viewing the sky, the former important constellation had disappeared, had sunk into an invisible sea, and a new one had risen. A former "age" had ended, and a new one had begun, with a new planetary ruler god. The objective astronomical reality was described in the myths of a flood which ended the old age. Santillana and von Dechend found this same basic myth everywhere, across the whole Earth. They traced it through Iceland, across Europe, Asia, the Pacific Islands, and the Americas. Only the elite, the educated astrologer priests, knew the actual astronomical source of the flood myths. "Ordinary" people assumed that they described historical facts — real floods. The western *Bible*'s version is the story of Noah.

Sullivan's book explores the related myths found in the cultures of the Andes, from the great city of Tihuanaco at Lake Titicaca which was a religious center several hundred years BC, to the Incas who were conquered by the Spanish in 1532. Sullivan's time table for the Aymara people of Tihuanaco is questionable. Alan Kolata's book *Valley of the Spirits*, published by John Wiley & Sons in 1996, claims that the kingdom of Tihuanaco lasted until after 1000 AD when it was hit by a severe drought that lasted for close to 400 years. The marvelous irrigation system developed by the people of the area was not able to function during the prolonged drought, the city was abandoned, and people dispersed. The ancient farming technique was rediscovered by modern archaeologists. It is now being practiced by current descendants of the Aymara in the Lake Titicaca area of Bolivia

Despite the questionable data on the Aymara dates, Sullivan's book is well worth reading. It is as fascinating as a detective story as he explains his efforts to penetrate the astrological meaning behind the symbolism in a variety of myths. One of the important conclusions from his work is the likelihood that the basic conceptual system which included precession was brought to the Andean people from the north, not independently invented. Sullivan points out close parallels between myths of the Andean area and the recorded myths of the Mayas and Aztecs. Especially significant is the fact that even though the Andean peoples lived south of the Equator, they maintained the system developed in the northern hemisphere in which north was up and south was down. Had the astrological system been locally developed, the reverse would have been more logical with the longest day of the year coming in December and the shortest in June.

I can't do justice to a very stimulating book, but it sent me on a search to explore astrological techniques which were used in the ancient world but which I had never tested. I knew of the former importance of the "fixed" stars, especially of stars which rise just ahead of the Sun — the so-called heliacal rising. The Egyptians were able to anticipate the flooding of the Nile and plant their crops when Sirius rose just ahead of the Sun. Sullivan interprets Andean myths to describe the people's dismay when, due to precession, the Sun no longer rose in the Milky Way on the June solstice. The Milky Way to the Mayas as well as to the Andean people was the bridge to the lands of the gods. The home of the gods was in the north, and they came to bless the people across the Milky Way at the June solstice. The home to which the human dead went during the interval before reincarnation was to the south, and at the December solstice, the dead returned to be welcomed with food and prayed to for help for the living. Halloween is our modern remnant of the ancient day when the dead returned to visit and eat with the living. The connection of the Milky Way to the December solstice lasted some 800 years longer than it did to the June solstice, but it too was lost in time, to the dismay of the people.

Sullivan describes a story told to the Spanish by local informants. A ruling Inca when they were still a relatively small tribe reportedly had a vision at about the time when that last bridge to the lands of the gods was lost. He was said to have predicted that within five generations, the Incas would lose their religion and their power. It was after this time, in the middle of the 1400s, that the Incas began their effort to conquer other groups. There is evidence of human sacrifice in every group which attained sufficient size and wealth to build monuments and maintain both an artisan and an elite noble class. But in the plus or minus 100 year period of the Inca rise to power, human sacrifice was expanded. Literally thousands of unblemished 10 and 11 year old boys and girls were killed each year. Theoretically, they were sent to intercede with the gods, to save the people from their anticipated disaster. Sullivan says: The gods answered. They sent the Spanish.

Sullivan points out the connection of the 800 year periods to the conjunctions of Jupiter and Saturn. As all astrologers know, these conjunctions occur at roughly 20 year intervals, and they were considered highly important keys to world events in the ancient world. In approximately 800 years, or 40 conjunctions, the planets would meet again in approximately the same place in the zodiac. This is the source of the common use of the number "40" in ancient stories, whether the 40 days that Jesus spent in the wilderness, or the 40 years in which the Israelites wandered in the wilderness. It is a general symbol for the completion of a cycle, and, like all myths, should not be taken too literally.

The mistake made by people who lacked knowledge of the astronomical/ astrological source of such numbers and of the cycles of precession, has been to take as literal facts the mnemonic (memory aiding) stories that were once told to the "peasants" by the educated elite. And, who knows whether anyone really understood the factual basis of the myths by the time the religious system reached the western hemisphere? Santillana and von Dechend think that Plato understood the source of the stories when he wrote about Atlantis as a way to describe his version of a properly conducted government, but the knowledge might have been lost (again) soon after him.

I think that many people with some psychic ability have created astral versions of these stories of civilizations going down into the sea. Edgar Cayce gave a major boost to the myth of Atlantis, helping to firmly establish it in the astral level, just beyond the physical world in which we are currently living. Anyone who can remember a dream can visit the astral Atlantis and add his or her own details to it. And, the more we visualize the apocalyptic scenarios, the more "solid" they become on the astral level, and the easier it is for people with a little psychic ability to experience them.

I think that the astral level is full of heavens and hells created by human minds; "happy hunting grounds," paradises where males can have all the beautiful houris they can imagine, little exclusive heavens where self-righteous believers can look down and see imaginary victims being tortured by the devil, and whatever else a fertile mind can create. Fortunately, the physical world is not so malleable to our psychic imagination, but our beliefs can certainly produce discomfort in our lives. Believers may quit their jobs, sell their homes, even leave their families, seeking safety from anticipated geological threats, but they lack the power to produce them in the material world. If living minds created earthquakes, we would have to conclude that fish have a lot of mind-power since there are many more earthquakes in the oceans than on land. I think our character creates our destiny. If we have an "earthquake character," we can move to a place where one will occur, but fortunately, we can't create it in the physical world. When dealing with our fellow humans, if Sullivan is right, the Incas killed a lot of children as a consequence of a destructive set of beliefs.

In addition to the books by Santillana, von Dechend, and Sullivan, David Ulansey's book on the Mithraic mysteries connects this mysterious religion to astrology and the precession of the equinoxes. For many years, Cumont's work on Mithraism was accepted as definitive, seeing the religion as simply a later and slightly revised form of the beliefs of ancient Persia. Though Ulansey does not mention it, Cumont, like many students of the ancient world, probably shared the pervasive bias against astrology held by western science, so he discounted the obvious indications that Mithraism was one of many variations of an astrological religion. It was even more successfully secretive than others of the related mystery cults which flowered in the

Graeco-Roman world during some hundreds of years preceding the beginning of Christianity. The Eleusinian and Orphic mystery religions originated earlier among the Greeks and/or their contemporaries in Asia Minor. Mithraism was a later Roman era faith among others which are less well known. All had beliefs and rituals which were only open to initiated members who were sworn to secrecy, so just fragments of their systems remain, often reported by hostile members of rival faiths.

Ulansey points out that Mithraism was especially successful in guarding its esoteric doctrines so almost no literary evidence remains, but because the rituals were mostly held in caves or underground temples, their contents were often preserved for later study by archaeologists. The temples provide a very rich iconography of statues and paintings which portray the beliefs once the symbols are interpreted. To anyone open to astrology, it is obvious that it was the foundation of the religion. The zodiac is a major theme, pictured in almost all of the temples along with the sun as either the god Helios or Apollo. Ulansey's book offers a convincing interpretation of some of the less obvious symbols consistently found in the temples.

The scene located in the central cult-niche in all of the temples portrayed Mithras killing a bull. Other figures were typically also shown, including a snake, a dog, a scorpion, a raven, and a cup. The relevant constellations are Hydra, Canis Major, Scorpio, Corvus, and Crater. Starting in the 1970s, other scholars began to question Cumont's interpretation of Mithraism, pointing out that these figures could picture the constellations which lie on or below the celestial equator between Taurus (the bull) and Scorpio (the scorpion). Also often pictured were a lion-headed man (Leo)and a sheaf of wheat (which could refer to Virgo or the star, Spica). The work of a German scholar named Stark was re-discovered. In 1869, Stark had suggested that the Mithraic bull-killing scene was a star map, but Cumont had rejected the theory despite his admission that the signs of the zodiac, the symbols of the planets, and the emblems of the elements appeared repeatedly in the Mithraic temple paintings and carvings.

Two human figures carrying torches often flanked the central scene, one with his torch pointing up and a bull's head associated with him, and one with his torch pointed down and an associated scorpion. Both figures were standing but had one leg crossed in front of the other leg. Similar figures called Dioscuroi had been included in earlier Greek mystery religions. To condense a long story into a few sentences, Ulansey suggests that the torchbearers represented the equinoxes which occurred formerly in front of the constellations of Taurus and Scorpio, but at the time when Mithraism developed, they had moved to the constellations of Aries and Libra. The crossed legs represented the intersection of the ecliptic and the equator. Though the ancient astrologers did not understand the ecliptic as the path of a moving earth, they were well aware of the two major circles around which the sky revolved.

Mithraism seems to have originated in the second century before the birth of Christ in the province in Asia Minor called Cilicia. It was largely a religion of soldiers and sailors, including the famous Cilician pirates. The latter were not a mere band of thieves. They were said to have numbered at least 20,000, in effect a small nation which at its height controlled the entire Mediterranean Sea. The Roman writer Plutarch claimed that many men with wealth and power cooperated with the pirates who commanded over 1000 ships and captured some 400 cities. It took three campaigns by Rome to finally wrest the Mediterranean Sea from their dominance. Mithraism was clearly a religion of power, only open to men and spread by its soldier and sailor devotees throughout the Roman Empire, even reaching the British Isles.

The theory advanced by Ulansey is that the religion originated in Tarsus, the capital of Cilicia, following the discovery (I think re-discovery) by Hipparchus of the precession of the equinoxes. Ptolemy was born very close to the death of Hipparchus, and he described how the latter deduced precession by comparing his own observations of the stars with those of an earlier astronomer named Timocharis. Tarsus was a renowned center of intellectual activity, especially noted for its famous Stoics including Hipparchus and Posidonius. The Stoics were firm believers in a fatalistic astrology in which the stars ruled all and the best that humans could do was to accept their fates with stoicism. The widespread astral religion had previously alternated between assigning supreme power to the Sun or to the current ruler of the gods who changed in the different "ages," but many serious philosophers believed that the realm of the "fixed stars" must be the ultimate power. Ulansey postulates a revelation experience by Hipparchus following the realization that the stars were not fixed but that the whole sphere moved over millennia of time. With the Stoic belief that there was a god associated with each basic force of nature, the God who could move the "fixed stars" must be the supreme power in the cosmos. Propitiating him would logically gain power and security for his worshippers, both in this world and in any other which followed death. Keeping the knowledge secret would be logical to maintain a monopoly on this source of power.

Parts of Mithraism were, as Cumont recognized, built on Persian roots, including the name of the all-powerful cosmic ruler, Mithras. In the bull-killing scene, Mithras is almost always pictured in a Phrygian cap with its bent top. This cap was associated with the east, and especially with Persia, but it also was worn by Perseus in the constellation that was visible in the sky directly over Taurus. Perseus not only was pictured in a Phrygian cap but he also held a short sword similar to the one being used by Mithras to kill the bull, and he was the patron god of Tarsus which evidence points to as the originating source of Mithraism. To the ancient world, gods controlled the forces of nature and also were associated with specific tribes, cities, and nations, as Yahweh was originally the tribal god of the Jews.

The belief in a newly discovered god who was powerful enough to shift the cosmos, to end the age of Taurus, the period during which the sun at the spring equinox was in front of the constellation of Taurus, could have led to an identification of this cosmic ruler with the patron god of the city of his discovery. The association would be supported by the constellation of Perseus in the sky in a dominant position over the bull. There was an intimate alliance between the Cilician pirates and the Mithridates dynasty whose rulers were named after Mithras and mythically descended from Perseus. Ulansey suggests this may have contributed to the pirates adopting the name Mithras for the new god. A series of rulers of Pontus used the name Mithradates and claimed descent from Perseus. Early in the first century BC, they conquered most of Asia Minor in alliance with the Cilician pirates. Pompey finally defeated them around 66 BC.

The Greek versions of the myth of Perseus make him an example of the widespread stories of a hero who kills a dragon. Perseus killed the gorgon, Medusa, who was so frightful that anyone looking at her was turned to stone. Perseus was successful with the help of magic tools which Athena and Hermes provided or told Perseus where they could be obtained. The tools included winged sandals which let him fly, a helmet which made him invisible, a mirror which let him approach Medusa without looking directly at her, a magic curved sword to cut off Medusa's head, and a magic bag to hold her head afterwards. Many of the Mithraic temples had representations of a lion-headed man whose head also resembled Medusa with snakes for hair. Much earlier versions of the dragon-killer existed in Sumerian stories where Marduk killed Tiamat.

An astronomical connection with the lion when it was portrayed in a power position is the fact that Leo is culminating in the sky when Taurus is setting. During much of the "age of Taurus," the solstices were in Leo and Aquarius while the equinoxes were in Taurus and Scorpio. But if this interpretation of Mithraism is accurate, its followers believed that the supreme cosmic ruler held power over all of the constellations. The Stoics already accepted the traditional belief in a series of "Ages" which included a golden age ruled by Chronos (the Roman Saturn,) the slowest of the visible planets, that was followed by the silver age of Zeus (Jupiter to the Romans). Greek writers prior to 500 BC mention this tradition, and paintings in Mithraic temples picture Chronos handing power over to Zeus.

Based on his limited information, Hipparchus calculated a time period of 36,000 years for the cosmic structure to revolve around the Earth. This newly recognized motion was in addition to the obvious daily rotation of the stars around Earth.

The two great circles were, as we know now, the ecliptic and the equator, but the ancient world had long differentiated the paths of the planets along the ecliptic from the paths of the stars around the pole of the equator. The big remaining question is whether Hipparchus was actually the first astrologer to recognize the fact of precession or just another in the history of human thought during which knowledge has been repeatedly gained and lost again.

The information presented by Santillana, von Dechend, and Sullivan, suggests that the knowledge of precession was acquired long before the Roman era, though probably always held as a secret by the educated Priests. The massive and fascinating book on the constellations by Sesti suggests that the formulation of the groups of stars into the traditional constellations with their accompanying myths may date to as early as 4,000 BC, and that it occurred in the Near East around 35 to 40 degrees north latitude. Sesti points out that when we take precession into account, the constellations which now seem inexplicable, upside down, and distorted, once formed orderly figures marking the boundaries of astronomical great circles and the dates which were so important to the ancient world, the equinoxes and solstices.

Three immense serpents are especially striking. Draco coiled at the top of the sky, holding both Thuban, the north polar star of that period and also the center of the ecliptic. Hydra stretched below the zodiac constellations of Cancer, Leo, Virgo, and Libra and it was centered in the sky at midnight on the winter solstice with its entire length on the celestial equator. It took 7 of the 24 hours of a day for it to pass the meridian. The serpent held by Ophiuchus also followed the celestial equator until it intersected the meridian of the fall equinox. It then bent in a right angle and followed the meridian until it marked the zenith with the star placed on its head.

The first known writing dates from Sumeria in the fertile valley through which the Tigris and Euphrates rivers ran to the Red Sea, and the earliest known myths of the Sumerians point to astronomical sources. Sargon, the Akkadian king who conquered the Sumerian city states around the middle of the third millennium BC, described Thuban, the current pole star, as the judge or crown of Paradise. The pole in mythology was the trunk of a tree and the stars were its fruits, commonly called apples. A cross section of an apple shows a five-pointed star. The stars were always associated with wisdom and a snake or dragon was usually their guardian. The myths differed in different cultures from the Garden of Eden in which the serpent encouraged Eve to eat the apple of knowledge (e.g. to study astrology), to the killing of dragons by human or divine heroes in order to release the sequestered knowledge to humans, to the punishment of humans who defied the gods to acquire their monopolized knowledge. Knowledge is power. Early Mesopotamian boundary stones have been found marked with the three celestial serpents, and with the same symbols for the lunar nodes that remain in use today. Humans learned to predict eclipses when the Sun and Moon were close to the ecliptic dragon, and the Moon's crossings of the ecliptic are still called the Head and Tail of the Dragon.

The importance of the sky as a clock has been mentioned, but it became especially important after the development of agriculture. The stone circles found from the Mediterranean islands to the British Isles testify to the immense labor undertaken by humans to let them pinpoint the "corners" of the circle, the solstices and the equinoxes which marked the annual seasons. On these days, the relative lengths of day and night changed. Gordon's book *Before Columbus* includes a map showing the distribution of megalithic (large stone) monuments from Asia Minor to the northeast Atlantic. Structures have been found in Malta, Sardinia, Minorca, Majorca, Spain, Portugal, Brittany, Denmark, England, and Ireland. The spread of a "megalithic culture" points to the spread of an accompanying astrological religion from its roots in the Near East to the edges of the world as it was known at the time. As one of many examples provided by Gordon, he cites a distinctively Mycenaean dagger which was carved on a megalith at Stonehenge, showing contacts at least as early as 1500 BC between the Aegean Sea region and Britain. An article by Mark Rose describes more recent work by archaeologists in Malta. Human habitation has been dated from 5000 BC and the villagers at that time had sheep, goats, cattle, pigs, wheat, barley, and lentils. Collective burials were found dating from 4200 to 3800 BC, and the first megalithic structures came soon afterwards, from 3600 to 3,000 BC.

Whole libraries of books have been written about the most famous of the megalithic monuments, Stonehenge in England. Theories about it range from dismissing the site as just a market for the surrounding countryside to seeing it as a sophisticated "computer in stone" which enabled its builders to predict eclipses. Stonehenge was built in stages and authorities still differ on precise dates. Stover and Kraig put its starting date at about 3000 BC while Hawkins dates its first stage to about 2200 BC with its last construction taking place about 1700 BC. By 1400 BC the structure was apparently abandoned. The increasingly later dates for the great stone structures as we move from the eastern Mediterranean to Britain strongly suggest that the beliefs which produced the incredible effort required to move the giant stones were carried from east to west, probably by migrating people. Though some archaeologists challenge Hawkins' interpretation of the astronomical knowledge possessed by the builders of Stonehenge and the hundreds of lesser stone circles found throughout the world, there is no doubt that they were astrological calendars, designed to at least identify the solstices and equinoxes.

As the title of his book suggests, Cyrus Gordon provides impressive evidence for contacts between a variety of early civilizations throughout the world, including contacts between the ancient Mediterranean region and the Americas. Though he dismisses astrology as a superstition, he acknowledges its pervasive influence throughout the ancient world. For example, he mentions evidence for contacts between ancient Crete and Egypt provided by the similarities in the zodiac on the Phaistos disc from Minoan Crete in about 1500 BC and the much later Dendera zodiac in Egypt. Despite a sizable collection of evidence for early diffusion from the "old" world to the "new" one, presented by many authors in addition to Gordon, orthodox archaeology still rejects such contacts. All parallel technology is still being credited to independent invention, despite discoveries like a sunken Roman ship in the harbor of Rio de Janeiro, Brazil. The response of the Brazilian government was to rebury the underwater ship, telling Robert Marx, the U.S. scuba diver who was led to it by local divers, that their official position was that Brazil was discovered by Portugal. The Brazilian Minister of Education told Marx "Every plaza in Brazil has a statue of Cabral, the real discoverer of Brazil, and we are not going to replace these with monuments to some anonymous Italian pizza vendor just because you have invented a Roman shipwreck where none exists." P.322

For astrologers, the most fascinating material in Gordon's book is his evidence that the alphabet developed by the Phoenicians originated from the lunar calendar of astrology. After the decline of the power of Minoan Crete around 1500 BC, the Greeks living on some of the islands and near the coast in Greece plus the Semitic Phoenicians living on the coasts of the eastern Mediterranean Sea, became the major sailors and traders of the area. Writing had existed in Mesopotamia from at least 3500 BC and in Egypt for almost that long, but it involved memorizing hundreds or thousands of characters which took years of study and was limited to a few professionals. Sailors needed a simpler system to keep track of the products they carried and the possible lengths of trips between ports. Late Bronze Age texts found in the Phoenician town of Ugarit in Asia Minor included Babylonian cuneiform, Egyptian and Hittite hieroglyphics, the Aegean syllabary, and the native Ugaritic alphabet.

Gordon follows up work by Hugh Moran and David Kelley connecting astrological calendar signs with the alphabet. By about 1400 BC, the Ugaritic alphabet had 29 signs with a phonetically superfluous 30th sign which corresponded with the length of the lunar month that vacillates between 29 and 30 days. The first letters of the names of the individual days in the lunar month became the letters of the alphabet. For example, the letter "b" came from bet which was a house, "g" came from gimil, "d" from dalet, etc. Gordon has a table aligning the alphabets of Ugarit, Hebrew-Phoenician, Greek, and Latin, demonstrating that the equivalent letters remained in the same order and even matched in the numerical values associated with the letters. The Hebrew numerical equivalents to the letters matched each succeeding letter with the numbers from one to ten. The following letters matched the numbers 20, 30, 40 etc. to 100 and then jumped to match the last letters with 200, 300, and 400. Alphabets are based on the principle that each unique sound or phoneme in a language is matched with a single unique symbol. When the Arabs took over the alphabetic principle and adjusted it to their own phonetic requirements, they rearranged the order of the letters drastically, but retained the old numerical values of every letter that exists in the Hebrew alphabet.

Though the evidence is more questionable, Gordon also suggests that the Mayan and Aztec calendar day names in their months were disseminated from the old world with some revised to fit local animals. Gordon's examples match the meanings of the ancient Phoenician letters with the Mayan and Aztec day names for water, house, hand, head, mouth, tooth, fish, etc. He is especially impressed by the fact that some sequences are repeated, such as k-l-m remaining in that order. Whether or not a connection is eventually confirmed between the Phoenician lunar calendar/alphabet of the old world and the calendar day names of the new world, Gordon calls this development of the alphabet a miracle of human ingenuity. In a single device, it provided a calendar to keep track of the days of the month, a system of arithmetic, and a phonetic alphabet which made writing and reading available to the masses, not just a tiny educated elite.

Calendars are circular, so the end of one cycle is the beginning of another, unless we believe in an apocalyptic scenario. The Mayans actually had a complicated system with more than one calendar; a ritual one of 260 days and a solar one of 18 twenty-day months with an extra five days at the end which were much feared as possible times of disaster. Scholars continue to debate the source of the ritual calendar. One guess connects it to the human gestation period. But the most reasonable theory I have seen comes from a geographer named Vincent Malmstrom in a recent book called *Cycles of the Sun and Mysteries of the Moon.* Malmstrom discovered that in the ancient ceremonial site of Izapa, in the region of Soconusco on the Mexican Pacific coast, the interval between the two days when the sun was directly overhead was precisely 260 days. At

Izapa, the sun was south of its overhead position for thirteen sets of 20-days and north for eight sets of 20 days. Evidence also supports Izapa being a site where the solar calendar was formalized, since at sunrise on the summer solstice, June 22, a viewer there sees the sun rise out of the highest volcano in Central America, Tajumulco. The solstices mark the "turning points" of the sun along the horizon and, as suggested in Sullivan's work, for many cultures they were more important than the equinoxes. The passage of the Moon in front of the constellations could be easily noted and early calendars were mostly lunar, but the brightness of the Sun blotted out the stars.

Archaeological evidence suggests that a previous, simpler community in the Soconusco region was impacted around 1500 BC by invaders from Ecuador in South America. Soon after that time, maize became the dominant source of food, and a calendar was needed to plant when the rains would come to germinate the seeds but would not be so strong that the seeds would be washed away. The ritual calendar did not stay in synchrony with the seasons, but it continued to be used as a base for religious ceremonies. Malmstrom calculated that the two calendars were developed at Izapa within a span of 30 to 35 years. It is known that the first day of the secular calendar was 1 Pop. Each of the 20 days in the "month" was named, and 1 Pop occurred on the summer solstice during the years 1324 to 1321 BC, using the Goodman-Martinez-Thompson correlation of Mayan dates with our modern calendar. The two calendars meshed and started a repetition of the name combinations every 52 years. The Aztecs had a similar system, undoubtedly borrowed from earlier cultures.

Our knowledge of the past, like most fields of knowledge, continues to expand. The jungles of northern South America remain largely unexplored and they undoubtedly still hide much information about the roots of civilization in the Americas. The *San Diego Union Tribune* on November 9, 1997 had an article about the finding of a "lost city" in northern Peru's Amazon rain forest. It was described as a pre-Incan stone city, built on slabs of stone and larger than the nearby pre-Incan Gran Pajaten which dates back to 2,000 BC. Gran Pajaten was only discovered in 1965, and little is known about the people who lived there. The Pacific coast of Mexico and Central America has also been studied less by archaeology than many other regions. An article in the November-December 1997 issue of *Archaeology* offers support for Malmstrom's suggestion that early little known people in Ecuador might have been a source of culture for people on the west coast of Mexico. Robert Pickering wrote that unlooted tombs have only recently been found and investigated by archaeologists, with some dating to around 2,000 years ago. Another article by Patricia Anawalt in the same issue of *Archaeology* offers evidence of parallels in dress and artifacts showing that strong economic ties existed between Ecuador and west Mexico more than 1500 years ago.

Malmstrom presents evidence that the mysterious Olmecs, who have been credited as the source of much of the culture taken over by the early Mayans, originated in the Soconusco region of west Mexico. He also explains that their earliest ceremonial site at San Lorenzo on the Gulf coast of Mexico was chosen partly to anchor their solar calendar. There were no dramatic mountain peaks to the north as there had been at Izapa, and the best one to the south was southwest, so they had to shift from the summer to the winter solstice and from sunrise to sunset. The site of San Lorenzo let them time a "turning point" of the sun by its setting position on the winter solstice.

If Malmstrom is right, the original source of the cultures of Soconusco and the Olmecs, both Zoque speaking peoples, comes from South America where archaeology has traced advanced civilizations to periods before 5,000 BC. It remains uncertain whether these advances were developed there or brought in from as yet unknown regions. Malmstrom believes that the calendars were developed in the Soconusco area, and Sullivan's work described earlier supports the importance of the solstices in the cultures of western South America. Malmstrom thinks that the concept of zero was developed with the calendars since days were counted only when they ended, so the first day of a cycle did not exist until it was finished. It was thus zero and the last day in the "month" was 19. The beginning of writing may also stem from Soconusco, but the Mayans may have vastly expanded it. Or could some of the ideas, though perhaps not the details, have come from the "old world," from the Near East? Will new work in Central America and northern South America finally support the evidence for contacts long before Columbus?

If Malmstrom is right, the Olmec culture came up from Ecuador and made a stunning intellectual breakthrough on the west coast of Mexico, but its most studied sites which have been excavated by modern archaeologists lie on the east coast near Vera Cruz and its hieroglyphics remain untranslated. Among the most fascinating remnants of the Olmec culture at its best-known sites of La Venta and San Lorenzo are giant heads carved of stone and weighing as much as 20 tons which have distinctly Negroid features. There is ample evidence from early Greek historians that, in addition to their colonies along the north coast of Africa, Phoenician sailors reached the Atlantic and traded with people living along the Atlantic coast of Africa. Some evidence supports their completely circling the continent. African natives may well have accompanied some of their ships and could have reached the Americas in Phoenician ships. Might some have remained in America to be worshipped as gods for their superior knowledge?

Malmstrom rejects the diffusion of culture from the old world to the new, opting for independent invention, but the evidence of Gordon, Marx, and others is impressive and only future research can resolve the controversy and answer many uncertainties. For those interested in the early cultures of Mesoamerica and in a unique theory describing their intense focus on astrology as they struggled to formulate a reliable calendar, Malmstrom's book is well worth reading! It must be said that the current official position of mainline archaeology is that Izapa was a later offshoot of the Olmec culture. They believe that its main center was the region of San Lorenzo and La Venta, but since earlier stages of development have not been found in this region, they may yet be found in other areas.

Returning to the "old world," relatively recent archaeological work has discovered stunning new information on a Near Eastern culture which reached its zenith in the middle of the third millennium. The name of Ebla appeared in early cuneiform writing in cities throughout the fertile crescent during a span of well over a millennium, but archaeologists did not locate and identify the buried remains of the city until the 1970s. For some hundreds of years during the third millennium BC, Ebla, located in current Syria, handled the pervasive rivalry between the early Sumerian and other Mesopotamian city-states through alliances, with the help of hired mercenaries, and by sheer commercial power. At its height between 2600 and 2500 BC, Ebla exercised power over most of Mesopotamia including part of Sumeria, but eventually it fell to one or possibly to a coalition of its Sumerian rivals. Its Italian excavator, Pettinato, has provided a fascinating description of the civilization of Ebla whose business, according to the author, was business.

The city was on primary trade routes which ran east and west between Sumeria and the Phoenician cities along the Mediterranean coast, and north and south between Anatolia and Egypt. Ebla's wealth and power were based on industry, especially textiles and metal working, and on trade, rather than on agriculture or domestic animals. Like Crete, women had more power than was customary in the ancient world. They worked for pay in the textile mills, not as slaves or servants. The "king" and the primary administrator of the society were elected at seven year intervals, and former "kings" and their families functioned as advisors. At its height according to its own records, Ebla included 17 countries with 2889 cities; a true empire.

The most exciting find at Ebla was the state library of over 20,000 cuneiform tablets, more than had previously been found in Asia Minor from the whole third millennium BC. When Ebla was conquered, the palace was burned which baked and thus preserved the clay tablets. Many tablets remain to be translated, but the information available when Pettinato wrote his book suggested that Ebla's downfall came after a king and his son who followed him made a grab to maintain personal power for their family, to turn a partial democracy into a hereditary monarchy. Ebla remained an inhabited city well into the second millennium, but its power was gone. More information will probably be forthcoming as the cuneiform texts are translated. Hopefully, Syria will remain open to archaeologists.

Many of the archaeological sites in ancient Babylon (current Iraq) are being looted and their information lost.

The culture of the island of Crete flowered during the latter part of the third millennium and into the second millennium BC. If its artwork can be trusted, it appeared to offer unusual respect and power to women. Priestesses were more frequently pictured than priests, and a female goddess was honored. There were few cities with walls and few signs of armed forces. In its island position, it had the sea as its protecting wall until other peoples developed the ships and the knowledge to challenge it. The main palace/temple in Crete's principle city, Knossos, was severely damaged, probably in an earthquake about 1700 BC, but afterwards it was rebuilt.

According to Castleden, the major downfall of the culture came after 1500 BC following a series of earthquakes which culminated in the monster quake that destroyed the nearby island of Thera in approximately 1470 BC. The consequences on Crete included structural damage from the quake and a tidal wave hitting the harbor towns on the north coast, and these were followed by a heavy rain of ash which would have put farmland out of production for several months. The Mycenaean invasion from Greece might have followed this disaster while Crete was weakened, though the conquest might not have been completed until the final burning of the palace and its so-called labyrinth in Knossos which is dated at about 1380 BC. The palace was not rebuilt after that.

Though much of the evidence from Crete suggests a relatively peaceful people, they did perform regular animal sacrifices, and at least one human sacrifice has been found. It probably dates from the earlier earthquake around 1700 BC, and may have represented an act of desperation in the face of the shaking earth. The Cretans major god, Poseidon, was both the god of the sea and also associated with earthquakes while the bull was his sacred animal. Crete is most famous for its paintings of individuals apparently somersaulting over the heads of bulls to land upright on the back of the bull. The dramatic scene found by archaeologists in 1979 was in a temple on a ridge overlooking the valley of Knossos. It included a 17 year old youth who had just been sacrificed and his blood drained to make an offering, and the two men and a woman who had officiated at the ritual had all died immediately afterwards when the roof of the temple fell on them as a result of a large quake.

Little has been said so far about the evolving cultures in Asia. There is ample evidence of trade between the ancient Near East and the Indus Valley in what is now Pakistan. The Harappan culture which developed along the Indus is best known for its sizable cities of Harappa and Mohenjo Daro, but there were also many smaller villages in the region. According to Wenke, people in the highlands above the valley had sheep and goats as early as 7000 BC. Agriculture, pottery, and copper tools were present in the valley by 3500 BC. By 2500 BC, the cities showed that the culture had evolved into a complex urban state. They had broad avenues, planned residential areas, and what may have been the most advanced municipal water and sewage system in the ancient world at that time, though Minoan Crete and the island of Santorini (Thera) which were at least partly contemporaneous also had impressive plumbing. The Harappan system included public toilets, drainage ditches along the main north-south street which was 9 meters wide, and individual homes of fired bricks had indoor showers with their plumbing connected to the public sewers.

The area influenced by the Harappan culture was bigger than any other Old World civilization at that time. Yet, in a brief 500 years, the major cities were abandoned though smaller villages continued. The Harappan hieroglyphics have not been translated, and the reason for the abandonment of the major cities remains a mystery. They may have suffered the fate of the fertile valleys of Mesopotamia which were frequently raided by nomadic herders from the surrounding hills and periodically conquered by aggressive tribes, often with the help of new weapons or military technology, but usually with a more primitive culture in other respects. Another theory postulates an earthquake which may have altered the path of or partially blocked the Indus river and flooded the agricultural fields which fed the people in the large cities.

Farther east in Asia, rice has been found in the Ganges plain in India as early as 4500 BC, and even earlier, at around 7000 BC, along the middle reaches of the Yangtze River in China. Millet was the main cereal grain in northern China. By the seventh to the sixth millennium there were villages in China with domesticated pigs and chickens as well as dogs which had become companions of humans far earlier. The earliest pottery vessels in the world have been found in Fukui Cave in Kyushu, Japan, dated to about 10,000 BC, but pottery also appeared in China at a very early date. The use of metal may have diffused from western and central Asia, though the Chinese developed their own distinct styles. Bronze was present by at least 2000 BC, but copper was in use much earlier. The carving of jade was an early specialty in China. New information being uncovered by archaeology in combination with historical written material is picturing a complex series of cultures and dynasties which evolved and sometimes fought and replaced others in the different regions of China.

Obviously, the timing of developing cultures was very different in different areas of earth, but perhaps we can end this brief archaeology/history survey with a list of generally accepted periods. The Paleolithic or "old stone age" is dated as running from around 1.4 million years ago to the end of the last ice age at about 11,000 BC. During this period, and still in some remote regions, humans lived in small, usually nomadic, bands surviving by hunting and gathering. During the Mesolithic or "middle stone age" from about 11,000 to 9000 BC, humans still depended almost entirely on hunting and gathering and the main signs of progress were the development of more effective stone tools. However, some agriculture may have been practiced in the Near East as early as 10,000 BC, very soon after the retreating glaciers of the last ice age accompanied a warmer climate. Recent work with the DNA of wheat points to the region of the Karacadag Mountains in Turkey as the probable origin of cultivated wheat about 10,000 years ago.

The generally accepted dates for the Neolithic or "new stone age" are from 9000 to 5000 BC. This period marked a major revolution as agriculture developed, probably out of the original gathering of wild seeds, animals were domesticated, settled villages became possible, and populations increased with a reliable source of food. Textiles, pottery, and metal tools became additional, valuable assets. There was never total security with the ever-present potential of droughts, floods, or raids by other villages or nomads looking for an easier way to gain possessions than by working for them. Most seriously, repeatedly there would be lasting invasions by tribes looking for a new home or by kings looking to expand the area they ruled. The grouping of homes into villages and the walls typically built around them were partly a response to the threats, though the village numbers also provided the manpower to build and maintain irrigation canals in areas with inadequate rainfall.

A variation on the division of the stone age into three parts came into general use in Europe though it was not helpful in the Americas. This system classified the period before the birth of Christ as a long Stone Age, followed by a Bronze Age, and lastly by an Iron Age. Copper was probably the first metal to be used for tools though both gold and copper were made into ornaments. There is evidence of copper use in Anatolia between 7000 and 6000 BC. Initially it was hammered and later humans learned to heat it and pour it into molds. The usefulness of metal was vastly increased when early metal workers learned to mix one part tin with ten parts of copper to produce bronze, a much harder metal which maintained a sharp edge and was easier to cast. Until recently, it was thought that the discovery of bronze might also have occurred in Anatolia not long before 3000 BC, but bronze has recently been discovered in Thailand dating to 3600 BC. As archaeology increases its reach to new areas, new information will undoubtedly be uncovered.

One theory suggests that an Indo-European group called the Hittites in Anatolia first learned how to work with iron though there are questions about both the people and the dates. Weapons and agricultural tools made with iron produced another quantum leap over bronze. Other Indo-Europeans, the Kassites, may have produced the first mobile war chariot pulled by a horse with one man controlling the horse and another shooting arrows or spearing the vulnerable foot soldiers. The Iranians are said to have initiated actually riding on horses, which again increased the ability to maneuver and threaten ground troops. The second millennium BC seems to have been noted for the increasing ability to wage war.

The primary facts of history during the centuries immediately before and after the birth of Christ are mostly tales of war and conquest. After the Greeks weakened themselves with the internecine Pelopponesian Wars, Alexander the Great swept out of Macedonia in northern Greece to take over virtually the whole "fertile crescent" of Asia Minor and Egypt, including an excursion as far as India. His dramatic rise to power and early death covered the short span of 13 years, from 336 to 323 BC. Following his death, his major generals divided the conquered territory among themselves.

Rome then increasingly dominated the Mediterranean world though they met their waterloo in the fierce tribes of central and western Europe. As usual, when a conquering power was on the march, the ordinary people in its path were killed or enslaved if they resisted and ruled and heavily taxed if they surrendered. Silberman's article on the time of Paul describes the impact of Roman rule on the spread of Christianity. He writes; "the world of Paul and the earliest Christians was affected by far-reaching economic dislocation, cultural conflict, and political change as formerly autonomous regions - from Spain to the Euphrates and from Britain to Upper Egypt - were linked by a centralized administration and increasingly regulated channels of trade." P. 32

Some of the areas where Paul preached most successfully were regions where Rome confiscated land from former owners and gave it to Roman citizens, including retired soldiers. Other recent authors have suggested that the original teachings of Jesus were politically subversive, not simply religious, and that Rome certainly regarded them in that light since only rebels against Rome were normally crucified. In a period of major stress, one of the primary reasons for the success of Christianity was their emphasis on members of the faith helping each other. The message of mutual support was far different from the Mithraic emphasis on power and its limitation of membership to men. Mithraism spread in the last part of the Arian Age. Christianity which replaced it was unquestionably a more appropriate faith for the Pisces Age. It is rather fascinating that both Mithraism and Paul who helped to defeat it were born in Tarsus.

To try to match this very abbreviated survey of early human culture with the astrological ages, we first need a timetable for the ages. As previously mentioned, the primary marker in the Near East was the movement of the vernal equinox in front of the constellations. Simultaneously, of course, the fall equinox and both solstices were moving in front of other star groups. I will list the dates for all of these "corners of the circle" during the most recent periods, but focus mostly on the vernal equinox in the search for correlations with human history. To avoid confusion, only the intervals marked by the vernal equinox will be called "ages." The periods during which the fall equinox and the solstices moved in front of the different constellations will be called "periods." A minus sign in front of a number indicates the number of years by which the date preceded the beginning of the Christian era. Since there is no zero year, a number preceded by the minus sign is one year earlier than a year which is labeled BC.

Vernal Equinox in front of the Constellations

Leo Age	-10519	to	-7792
Cancer Age	-7683	to	-6665
Gemini Age	-6358	to	-4774
Taurus Age	-4143	to	-1689
Aries Ave	-1854	to	-389
Pisces Age	-110	to	2817 AD
Aquarian Age	2691	to	5431

Summer Solstice in front of the Constellations

Leo Period	-4149	to	-1263
Cancer Period	-1148	to	-120
Gemini Period	299 AD	to	1753
Taurus Period	2373	to	4765

Fall Equinox in front of the Constellations

Scorpio Period	-4348	to	-2524
Libra Period	-2318	to	-1187
Virgo Period	-877	to	2475 AD

Winter Solstice in front of the Constellations

Gemini Period	-12533	to	-11074
Taurus Period	-10508	to	-8197
Aries Period	-8369	to	-6935
Pisces Period	-6640	to	-3705

The dates above mark the years when the equinoxes and solstices reached the first star and left the last star in each constellation. However, since the movement of precession is only about one degree in 72 years, picking a specific year for our calendar of the ages is really an approximation. If we allow an orb of even one degree, we would alter the dates by 72 years. Also, overlapping constellations can be conceptualized as marking a time of transition when the themes of both constellations are present, but there is no consensus on how to handle the constellations with open space between their end stars. We might divide the space between the two constellations or consider it a time for greater freedom; like a recess between classes. Obviously, the constellations differ widely in size, so the lengths of the "ages" also differ. The dates were calculated by Mark Pottenger and Robert Hand. The assignment of specific stars to the different constellations from which these dates were derived comes from the Alexandrian astrologer Ptolemy who lived in the second century AD. Essentially the same star groups have been used by humans for some 2000 years, though later astronomers have added new groups to modern star maps.

Our figures bring the vernal equinox to the first star of Leo in the middle of the 11th millennium BC as the last ice age was phasing out, and the Leo Age lasted through most of the Mesolithic period and well into the Neolithic. We associate Leo and fire in general with creativity, with the urge to do more than we have done before. Leo seems appropriate for the tremendous shift in the Near East from survival living by hunting and gathering to taking power over both plants and animals with agriculture and domestic herds. Populations increased as control was attained over the sources of food, and wealth grew with new possessions including pottery. Trade expanded along with the new technology. As early as 9500 BC humans were crossing the 62 miles of open sea between the island of Melos and south Greece to acquire obsidian, the volcanic rock valued for sharp stone tools. Jericho was a settled town before 9000 BC and by 8000 BC a wall had been built around it for security.

The constellation of Cancer is a short one, so the vernal equinox took less than a thousand years to move in front of Cancer. More settled villages, larger homes, new crops, and new techniques to attain comfort were being developed, probably including woven textiles and the beginning of work with metal.

Gemini is longer than Cancer, but its age was still considerably shorter than the 2000 year periods assumed by students who simply divide the approximately 26000 years of precession by 12 to determine the length of each age. This interval is too early for the first known writing in Sumeria, but the Chinese claim to have had written characters as early as 5500 BC.

There is a sizable gap between Gemini and Taurus, which obviously did not stop humans from continuing to expand their knowledge and power. The long Taurus Age brought the shift from prehistory which is gradually being revealed through archaeology to history which can be studied from written records. During this period of nearly 2500 years, some villages became nation-states and empires with increasing stratification into classes: elite, wealthy rulers at the top and slaves at the bottom. Wealth expanded enormously, from exquisite jewelry to such features as indoor plumbing in Crete, Santorini, and the Indus Valley. This was the period when the great stone structures were built from Asia Minor across the islands of the Mediterranean to the islands of Britain. The evidence is still fragmentary, but the odds are that a religion of astrology was the driving force behind the enormous investment of human energy. The bull figured prominently in religion, painted, carved, and modeled in figurines in the temples, but also sacrificed. Goddesses and priestesses were also important in many areas. In some cultures, including Crete and Ebla, women seemed to have had respect and personal rights.

The shift of the equinox from Taurus to Aries included an overlap period of about 165 years and it provides one of the most striking correlations with the historical record. From a Venus-ruled constellation, humans moved to Mars, the god of war. The villages of Sumeria had fought each other and outsiders almost from the beginning of settled life, and recent archaeological work in Spain has found early humans eating other humans before 800,000 BC. Mars was not needed to introduce aggression. But the ability to kill large numbers of people did expand in the second millennium BC with the help of iron weapons, chariots, and horses. Iron, the metal of Mars, replaced copper, the metal of Venus except for ornamental uses.

As discussed previously, at least two relatively peaceful cultures bit the dust. The major cities of the Harappan culture of the Indus Valley were abandoned for unknown reasons before the end of the Taurus Age, and even the villages which continued the Harappan culture seem to have disappeared during the transition period to the Arian Age. Santorini (Thera) was wiped off the face of the Earth and the volcanic explosion and earthquakes weakened Crete which was conquered soon afterwards by the Mycenaean Greeks from the mainland. Stonehenge was abandoned along with the building of great stone monuments. This may be the period when Zoroaster initiated the apocalytic ideas which remain pervasive.

On the credit side, the alphabet seems to have been developed near the beginning of the Arian Age, removing the monopoly on knowledge formerly held by a few educated elite, and trade continued to expand, possibly reaching the Americas. Whatever the eventual decision on their roots, the Olmecs seem to have initiated a new cultural phase in Mesoamerica around the middle of the first millennium. Greek city states continued to fight each other, yet during the Arian Age Greece also produced some serious philosophers and political experiments which are seen by many as the foundation of western civilization.

The gap between Aries and Pisces coincides with the Hellenistic period in Greece. It covers the conquests of Alexander, the brief reign of the Cilician pirates, and the early stages of Rome's rise to power. Obviously, a more thorough survey of history would specify many more details.

Astrologers do not need to be reminded that Christianity is Piscean. Jesus attracted fishermen to carry on his teachings and told them he would make them "fishers of men." One of his first reported miracles involved the multiplication of loaves and fishes and others took place on the fishing boats of his followers. A stylized fish was the symbol letting people know that a house belonged to members of the faith who could offer assistance. It is also featured in various ways in the garments and ritual objects carried by church officials. We are still far from practicing the Christian teaching of empathy and compassion, but fortunately we still have some hundreds of years to learn to be more Piscean.

The theories discussed so far suggest that the religious apocalyptic beliefs which seem to have been mostly born of wishful thinking by people under intense stress have been thoroughly mixed with a too literal interpretation of the ancient myths of cyclic ages based on the precession of the equinoxes moving in front of the constellations. But there is a third possible source of some of this mix. Several books were published in the 1950s to the 1960s by Immanuel Velikovsky, a psychoanalyst who proposed what the scientific world considered outrageous theories. His book *Worlds in Collision* published by Macmillan in 1950 became a best seller, but Macmillan received so much flak from "scientists" who threatened to boycott the textbooks it also published, that the company gave the rights of the book to Doubleday. The episode was a shocking illustration of the lack of objectivity among so-called scientists. Some of his fiercest critics actually bragged that they had not read his heretical book.

Velikovsky's research was actually very impressive, including predictions considered absurd at the time which were later found to be accurate such as radio noise emanating from Jupiter and a high temperature on Venus. In later books he described the extensive physical evidence of past catastrophes on Earth which killed huge numbers of animals and humans, and he noted the stories of rains of fire and stone, days of darkness, rivers of blood, etc. Velikovsky suggested that these catastrophes might have been caused by a comet, but he really upset the standard scientific belief system in a stable solar system by theorizing that the source of the destruction was actually Venus careening around the solar system and narrowly missing Mars and the Earth. He pointed out that in many early cultures, the same word was applied to Venus and to comets, and Venus was described as "long-haired, bearded," "smoking", etc. Later, on the strength of ancient myths about Saturn as ruler of a golden age, Velikovsky suggested in an unpublished manuscript that Earth was once a satellite of Saturn, and that this was recent enough to be retained in stories carried down to historical periods.

Alert readers will have noted that Egypt was conspicuously missing in the descriptions and dates for many ancient cultures. Archaeologists remain convinced that their dates for ancient Egypt are accurate, but the historical evidence presented by Velikovsky in his last three different books offers a real challenge to the orthodox time table. Rather than try to deal with extensive, technical, and very controversial information, I decided to omit Egypt even though it is certainly one of the most important keys to the evolution of human culture on earth. Starting in the 1950s, several new techniques were developed and became available to archaeologists. They provide "absolute" rather than simply relative dates for the past. Among these are radiocarbon, thermoluminescence and archaeomagnetic dating. In time, they will either support Velikovsky or the currently accepted dates for ancient Egypt.

For astrologers who are familiar with the widespread myths of the "Ages," it is obvious that Velikovsky had fallen victim to the problem previously discussed — taking literally what were myths based on precession. Part of the world-wide astrological belief system traced by *Hamlet's Mill* included the successive ages of Gold which was followed by Silver and then by Iron. Saturn was the original mythical ruler of the remote and idealized golden age in some versions, and he was deposed by his son, Jupiter to use their Roman names. To the Greeks, they were Chronos and Zeus. Saturn/Chronos was always associated with time. Jupiter and Saturn were the slowest planets, the farthest out as we know now, of the planets visible without telescopes. The conjunctions of Jupiter and Saturn every 20 years were major timers and keys to the world scene for the ancient peoples.

But early astrology was far from formalized into a logical system. In the association of metals with planets, Saturn was given lead and he was usually seen as the great malefic. Mars was second to Saturn as a threat to humans. In later more organized astrology, as humans continued to observe the patterns in the sky and to correlate them with events on earth, gold belonged to the Sun, silver to the Moon, and iron to Mars, the god of war. In the Near East where this effort was strongest, Venus was associated with copper and became the goddess of love, equated with Artemis, Aphrodite, and other goddesses. Naturally, the gods had different names in different cultures, but they referred to the same planets. Yet it is true that she was also assigned to Libra which could be a zodiacal sign of either partnership or warfare, and Venus could be pretty nasty in some of the Greek stories. She was not purely sweetness and light as some modern astrologers would like to believe. To the Mayans, Venus was one of the most feared of the planetary gods, and was definitely associated with war. Astrology was then, and remains, a work in progress.

The "scientists" attacking Velikovsky had some evidence on their side since early records of Venus, Mars, and Saturn show them in orbits which fit modern calculations projected into the past. The major planets in the solar system do seem to have been in stable orbits for a very long time. If Velikovsky had not taken astrological myths literally, and had stayed with his evidence for catastrophes coming from the sky in times recent enough for the traditions to be retained into historical periods, he would have been on solid ground. Over the years since the original Velikovsky "episode," his fame and acceptance has risen and fallen. A number of serious researchers have been impressed and have sought evidence to support his theories. One such group is currently presenting their ideas in a scientific journal published in England. They are also holding conferences to discuss the ideas which include very concrete and persuasive evidence specifying a precise source of past catastrophes. One of the leaders of this current group is Dr. Victor Clube in Oxford University, and they include searchers in Oregon, northern California, a man who works for NASA, and a University Professor in Australia among others.

Dr. Richard Heinberg sent me an article by Clube from the 1996 issue of *Vistas in Astronomy*. Dr. Heinberg was a personal assistant to Velikovsky in his last years, and he has continued to study and write on mythology, anthropology, and ecology. He publishes a small but very interesting monthly newsletter which is available from him for $15 a year in the U.S.. Write to him at: 1433 Olivet Road, Santa Rosa, CA 95401.

The Clube article is fascinating and wide-ranging, but so complex I can't begin to do justice to it. He summarizes a Spenglerian model of civilization, which is the title of his article, as an alternation in human history between a pre-Socratic view of the cosmos which was continued by the neo-Platonists and an Aristotelian conceptual belief system about the nature of ultimate reality. As Clube describes this alternation, the early belief systems pictured a Universe which is infinite in extent, both temporally and spatially, but with life here on earth subject to an astronomical environment which influenced or controlled it. (My addition: astrology was the basic religion of early humans).

Clube writes: Plato and his predecessors... "subscribed to the idea of innumerable worlds of 'cosmic eggs' scattered throughout infinite space which passed in and out of existence. The underlying idea was that of an infinite or 'boundless' Universe whose constituents therefore represented the unlimited 'stuff' of the Universe. Such 'stuff' was of an ungenerated and imperishable nature; it was also in a state of eternal motion, being therefore classified as immortal and divine." (My addition: In essence, as the religions of the east have put it, "we are that," part of the immortal infinite.) In Plato's terms, while here on Earth, we are part of a particular cosmic egg and they are finite, subject to beginnings and endings which are connected to the astronomical environment. (My addition: Many people believed that our world was controlled by what, to them, were the astrological gods of the sky.)

The Aristotelian conceptual system was closer to the one eventually accepted by Christianity — a finite Universe, both temporally and spatially, and subject to external, benevolent control. (My addition: Modern western science continued this system but removed any hint of divinity, made ultimate reality totally physical, and substituted "natural law" for God). Spengler suggested that in periodic times of crisis and change, humans switched from one of these basic belief systems to the other.

Clube, like all scientists who want to be accepted by the scientific community, has trouble dealing with astrology. He is trying to offer evidence to account for and to justify the total acceptance of astrology by the ancient world without admitting that there is any truth in the claims of modern astrology. His primary information which I found so exciting includes his evidence for previous impacts on earth by cometary fragments which affected the course of history, but he goes much farther!

The Alvarez theory that major extinctions of life on earth were caused by impacting asteroids or comets has now been generally accepted. Clube points out that occasional events such as the Tunguska explosion in Siberia in 1908 could justify fear of astronomical phenomena by early humans But Clube suggests that physically non-threatening phenomena such as unusual numbers of meteors (meteor streams), and eclipses, and comets which did not fragment and hit Earth, instilled such fear in humans that they produced revolutions in religions and politics. He tries to deny that astrology could be a valid key to life on earth while accounting for the universal fearful beliefs and reactions of humans in the past to astronomical phenomena. So, in the abstract of his article, he writes: "The historical fear of comets which has been with us since the foundation of civilization, far from being the reflection of an astrological perception of the cosmos which was deranged and therefore abandoned, has a perfectly rational basis in occasional cometary fragmentation events."

I am reminded of the cliché from Shakespeare — "Methinks thou doth protest too much." Of course, Clube, like most scientists, may never have seen competent modern astrology. Another cliché is "Never the twain shall meet." In general, occultists and scientists distrust each other. The belief system of each is threatening to the other. Their concepts are so different, in effect they speak different languages, so communication is truly difficult. But, even more, we live in our belief systems, so they are a primary source of our security. Most people react to a challenge to their beliefs as they react to an earthquake — with terror.

Clube's main theory is that fragments of comets have hit Earth repeatedly within the last few thousand years, creating terror in humans and changing cultures in dramatic ways. He suggests that even spectacular streams of meteors, which are presumably fragments of comets, could have produced fear and general social destabilization which resulted in revolutions. He connects the theories of Spengler and Toynbee, who described periodic violent crises in human history, with periods of increased astronomical phenomena - not just eclipses and occasional comets, but also fireball flux surges (meteors).

Chinese astronomers made exceptionally extensive records of astronomical phenomena, and Clube has noted correlations between increased unusual activity in the sky and many periods of unusual turmoil in human affairs. In line with the relatively new view of evolution that it remains static for long periods but then is punctuated with bursts of rapid change, Clube agrees with Spengler and Toynbee that this general picture also fits the evolution of human cultures. He associates episodes of increased fireball flux with the periods from 0 to 100 AD when Christianity was being formulated, 400 to 600 when the Roman Empire collapsed, 1040 to 1100 for the Crusades, 1400 to 1460 for the Great Schism, 1500 to 1540 for the Reformation, 1640 to 1680 for the English Revolution, and 1760 to 1800 for the American and French revolutions. His focus is obviously on western history, and more work will be needed to see whether other cultural areas were also destabilized at these times.

In addition to checking astronomical records in China and other countries, Clube also offers mathematical formulas in a search for repetitive patterns. He even pinpoints the remnants of what he thinks was the great comet responsible for some of the chaos in human affairs during the last 2,000 years; our present comet Encke and the Taurid-Encke meteor stream which is seen annually in July-August and October-November. Of course, with his basic belief in scientific materialism, Clube has to blame the turbulence of humans on their fear of coming disaster from the sky.   That seems almost bizarre to me, thinking that humans reform religions and fight wars and depose kings just because they are upset by meteors.   Logically, humans would not have remained so obsessed with the sky if meteors had come and gone while their lives remained stable.   But, those who believe that the world is inherently meaningless cannot consider the possibility that the events in the sky are a source of valid information rather than a cause.

As I have written in many previous books, I think that the sky is a visible part of the order of the cosmos so it is a convenient way to see the order. It does not create it.   Jung coined the term "synchronicity" to describe a meaningful coincidence.   The cosmos is evolving, in fits and starts as the punctuation theories suggest, and the sky offers us a map of the psychological issues at any given time and place; a mirror of the emotions which are driving us, a clock showing the timing for events in individual lives and in societies which are driven by those emotions.   The events are not caused by the sky, whether we metaphorically call it a clock or a model, or a mirror.   The events are the culmination of many prior causes; ripe destiny or karma in an endless chain until we change our emotional attitudes and actions.

So if I don't agree with their materialistic conclusions, why am I excited by the work of Clube and other astronomers who are finally recognizing a relationship between the sky and human actions, human history? Partly, because I find any new knowledge about the cosmos and humans exciting. *Hamlet's Mill*, Sullivan's book on the Incas, and the work of Gordon, Malmstrom, Velikovsky, Clube and others are reminders that there is always more to discover, "new to us" astrological techniques and insights that may help us understand where we came from, how we got here, and what we might do next. But more importantly, despite their disclaimers, Clube and his fellows are providing support for astrology in their correlations between astronomical phenomena and history.

I am not suggesting that early humans did not fear comets, eclipses, and unusual meteor streams. Written records provide ample evidence for that. I am saying the fear was based on astrological knowledge that disturbances in the sky typically accompanied disturbances on earth. I think that for millennia humans observed the correlations between drama in the sky and uproar on earth. Their fears were realistically directed at more mundane events than the remote chance of being hit by a fragment of a comet. Unusual turbulence in the sky did accompany wars, famine, pestilence, weather crises on earth such as droughts and floods, etc.

Nowadays, most educated people are too sophisticated to fear comets. Halley's comet was not much of a spectacle on its last return. Hale-Bopp has come and gone, without repercussions except for the suicides of some misguided "true believers" and red faces for some remote viewers. If its visit to the inner regions of our solar system coincided with any major turning points in human history, I missed them. A number of researchers are now theorizing that evolutionary breakthroughs occur when living beings are stressed. Clube's addition is the suggestion that unusual astronomical events have been in the past one of the major sources of such stress on humans. That is true as far as it goes. We just need to remember that the stress comes from the **beliefs** of the humans. If Sullivan is right, it was the beliefs of the Incas which led them to fear being cut off from their gods and to sacrifice thousands of children in the vain hope of persuading the gods to reconnect with and protect them.

The rise of materialistic science may have been necessary to break humans free from a lot of destructive beliefs. Science threw out the baby with the bathwater, and the efforts of Clube and others are a part of our current efforts to recover the baby without the dirty bath water. Astrologers are now challenged to sift out the valid and helpful insights of their theories from a lot of traditional and often destructive nonsense.

To summarize the preceding material, I think that all of these sources of human beliefs and fears are playing a role in the present millennial fever. As I write often, life is an "and," not an "either/or." Previous humans fought revolutions and created other turmoil as an outgrowth of accumulating frustrations plus, usually, some new ideas, **and** these turbulent times occurred when there were corresponding unusual patterns in the sky, **and** the widespread beliefs in astrology undoubtedly contributed to the general feelings of foreboding and willingness to consider radical action. Currently, some people pressured by economic and other fears are hoping for an end to such pressures, for a paradise providing all their desires without any challenges.

Many people take the myths literally, whether they accept the *Bible*, or the shamanic traditions of native people, or the pronouncements of psychic channelers or UFO abductees. The warnings of current versions of Malthus and Rachel Carson are also a source of concern to thinking people. Overpopulation, the destruction of ozone in the atmosphere and of the rain forests, global warming, soil erosion, pollution from damaging chemicals from industry and agriculture as well as nuclear waste and stock piles of nerve gas, are all serious matters which can add fuel to the fire of pervasive unease, not to mention the investment gurus predicting financial collapse.

What can we as individuals do? Serious students of astrology can continue to study the parallels of meaning between the sky and the affairs of earth, and to use the knowledge to handle life more effectively. We can work for or contribute to efforts to limit population growth and clear cutting of old growth forests, to protect endangered species, or for any other "cause" that appeals to us. We can **vote** for politicians who share our concerns. But I truly believe that part of our contribution can be expressing as much love and joy as we can muster. Character creates destiny. Character is habits which are carried over from one physical expression to another. Habits of love and joy not only create a better personal destiny; they help the world to move in that direction. I stand with the pre-Socratics. I think that ultimate reality is composed of emotion (desire/aversion) and information which life processes to facilitate movement toward what is desired and avoidance of what is not desired. As participating expressions of that eternal Infinite, we contribute to the manifestation of its unrealized potentials.

To test Sullivan's ideas about the solstices and the Milky Way, I ran a lot of charts for solstices and Jupiter-Saturn conjunctions from 204 BC to the coming of the Spanish in 1532, but in the end, the computer program *Dance of the Planets* was more helpful in demonstrating that Sullivan was approximately right in his dates on the loss of the "bridge to the worlds of the gods" at the June and December solstices when the Sun at the solstices no longer rose in the Milky Way.

I also ran a variety of charts to test the beliefs being promoted by some westerners that the end of the current Mayan "long count" calendar will mark an apocalyptic end of the world or at least of our age, but I was not impressed by any of them. As previously mentioned, some Mayans in relatively remote areas still believe that a catastrophic war is coming and that they will rule the world afterwards. December 21 or 22, 2012 are the dates normally cited for the end of the calendar, but I have not seen a time of day for this predicted event. The Sun will enter 0 Capricorn on the 21st, so I looked at that Capricorn Ingress which will occur at 11:13 UT, but the chart seemed unremarkable. The entry of the Sun into the cardinal signs is traditionally a key to the coming 3 months. If anything important is to occur during this interval, it should show in the horoscope. The chart is arbitrarily calculated for Palenque, a major center of classic Mayan culture, but if readers are interested in seeing the angles in other areas, they can make the minor mathematical adjustments I also looked at a chart for the next day, December 22, and it seemed appropriate to run the chart for sunset; the end of the day since the Mayas traditionally only counted a day when it ended.

The Sun will be on the Descendant at 17:35 CST. Jupiter in its own twelfth house will be quincunx both Saturn and Pluto in the sign of Saturn — a fitting pattern for religious illusions meeting the reality of this physical world, doing some analysis, and perhaps changing some of the beliefs. Repeating this message are a number of squares between the mutable signs and houses. A common form of the mutable dilemma is the conflict between beliefs and the reality of the world we live in.

I also did a chart for the reported beginning of the Mayan calendar which is described as the "birth of Venus." August 13, 3114 BC (or minus 3113 to use the alternate nomenclature) is the date given in both *The Mayan Prophecies* by Gilbert and Cotterell and *Maya Cosmos* by Linda Schele, David Freidel, and Joy Parker. Both books specify that the ancient Mayan date has been translated into the modern Gregorian calendar. To have a chart, we have to have a time of day as well as a place. So, I put Venus on the Ascendant which is traditionally the point of beginning life. As with the chart for 2012, this early horoscope is calculated for Palenque. I progressed the early chart to the previously mentioned date which is theoretically the end of the current cycle in 2012 AD. Fortunately (or unfortunately for the prophets of doom), the resulting patterns do not support a world-shaking change.

In addition to the current popularity of ancient Mayan beliefs, another reason for focusing on the Mayas is their obsession with Venus. Velikovsky's research connecting Venus to the appearance of comets and the Mayan fear of Venus makes one wonder whether the planet was somehow connected to an ancient catastrophe. Could one of the episodes when cometary fragments actually did widespread damage to Earth have occurred when Venus was prominent in some way? Maybe at heliacal rising, when the Mayans especially feared the planet, maybe conjunct the Sun, Mars, or Saturn, maybe on a solstice date or when the Sun was directly overhead which occurred twice each year in most of the Mayan region. Linda Schele discovered that August 13 was one of the days when the Sun was directly overhead in Copan and other important ancient Mayan cities. This is all speculation, but wouldn't we love it if a record carved on a stele were found!

As has been noted repeatedly, the importance of the sky was totally pervasive in the ancient world. Humans needed calendars for the practical business of planting maize and for the ritual propitiation of the gods who supposedly controlled the forces of nature - volcanic eruptions, earthquakes, floods, storms, etc. But calendars are circular. As already stated, the end of one cycle is the beginning of another, unless we believe in an apocalyptic scenario. I am bemused by the true believers who are convinced that primitive or ancient people were all enlightened. The archaeological evidence for human sacrifice as an integral part of a great many ancient religions should raise some doubts about the spiritual wisdom of the practitioners, but humans hungry for revelation can ignore evidence and common sense, create fantasies of doom and gloom, and look for a hill or a cave.

So, what do I think is reality? Everything! But there are an infinite variety of realities. To scientific materialists, only the physical is "real," but I think that emotional experiences, cognitive or intellectual experiences, and spiritual experiences are even more "real" in the sense that they are more inclusive, more universal, more enduring. We just need to recognize the different types of reality and not confuse them. That ability to discriminate may be the great gift of life in this physical world. The combinations of physical and cognitive reality which we can experience here let us make conceptual models of our experience and test them against the physical (and other) consequences.

What we think of as memories, though they usually contain fabricated components, plus imagination, fantasy, dreams, myths and other cognitive models are non-physical reality. We can lump them under the term "astral" or psychic while acknowledging that the levels or "realms" in the "astral" are undoubtedly more complex than we can imagine when we are operating in and mostly focused on this physical realm. Some gurus teach that we should focus on escaping from this physical level of experience. But why would the Infinite produce it and life explore and expand it unless it offered some value? Maybe sitting on a cloud and playing a harp just gets boring after a while. Maybe life is the urge to do more than we have done before, even though it is often painful. I think that pain is our warning signal of some type of excess when we have gone too far in one direction and lost other valuable parts of life. Astrology is the most useful of the many cognitive models of reality that I have explored, but it is still a model and no model is total and final truth. Even with astrology, life is still an experiment. We try something, in any level of reality, see what happens, then decide whether we want to continue doing it. Bon Voyage!

References

Anawalt, Patricia, "Traders of the Ecuadorian Littoral," *Archaeology*, November-December, 1997.

Bakich, Michael E., *The Cambridge Guide to the Constellations*, Cambridge University Press, Great Britain, 1995.

Bauval, Robert & Gilbert, Adrian; *The Orion Mystery*, Crown Publishers Inc, NY, 1994.

Bikai, Patricia M., "The Phoenicians," *Archaeology*, March-April 1990.

Boissiere, Robert, *The Return of Pahana*, Bear & Co, Santa Fe, NM, 1990.

Boyer, Paul, *When Time Shall Be No More*, Harvard University Press, Cambridge, 1992.

Brecher, Kenneth & Feirtag, Michael, EDs; *Astronomy of the Ancients*, The MIT Press, Cambridge, MA, 1979.

Bunson, Margaret & Bunson, Stephen, *Encyclopedia of Ancient MesoAmerica*, Facts on File, Inc, NY, 1996.

Castleden, Rodney, *Minoans*, Routledge, London, 1990.

Clube, S.V.M., "The Nature of Punctuational Crises and the Spenglerian Model of Civilization," *Vistas in Astronomy*, vol. 39, 1996.

Cohn, Norman, *Cosmos, Chaos & the World to Come*, Yale University Press, New Haven, 1993.

Fagan, Brian, *Kingdoms of Gold, Kingdoms of Jade*, Thames and Hudson, London, 1994.

Fagan, Brian, *Time Detectives*, Simon & Schuster, NY, 1995.

Fagan, Brian, Ed. *The Oxford Companion to Archaeology*, Oxford University Press, Oxford, England, 1996.

Freidel, David, Schele, Linda, Parker; Joy, *Maya Cosmos*, William Morrow & Co, NY, 1995.

Friedrich, Johannes; *Extinct Languages*, Philosophical Library, 1957 (reprint - Barnes & Noble, 1993).

Gardner, Joseph I., Ed. *Mysteries of the Ancient America*, Readers Digest, NY, 1986.

Gilbert, Adrian and Cotterell, Maurice, *The Mayan Prophecies*, Element, Great Britain, 1995.

Gordon, Cyrus H, *Before Columbus*, Turnstone Press Ltd, London, 1971.

Hawkins, Gerald S., *Beyond Stonehenge*, Harper & Row, NY, 1973.

Henderson, John S., *The World of the Ancient Maya*, Cornell University Press, Ithaca, NY, 1981.

Heyerdahl, Thor, and Sandweiss, Daniel, and Narvaez, Alfredo, *Pyramids of Tucume*, Thames and Hudson, London, 1995.

Kolata, Alan L., *Valley of the Spirits*, John Wiley & Sons, US, 1996.

Malmstrom, Vincent H., *Cycles of the Sun, Mysteries of the Moon*, University of Texas Press, Austin, TX 1997.

Marx, Robert F & Marx, Jenifer, *In Quest of the Great White Gods*, Crown Publishers Inc, NY, 1992.

Menzel, Donald E., *Field Guide to the Stars*, Houghton Miflin Co, Boston, MA, 1964.

Miller, Mary and Taube, Karl, *The Gods and Symbols of Ancient Mexico and the Maya*, Thames and Hudson, London, 1993.

O'Brien, Christian, *The Megalithic Odyssey*, Turnstone Press Limited, Wellingborough, Northamptonshire, 1983.

Pettinato, Giovanni, *The Archives of Ebla*, Doubleday & Co, NY, 1981.

Pickering, Robert B., "Discovering the Occidente," *Archaeology* Nov-Dec 1997.

Pringle, Heather, *In Search of Ancient North America*, John Wiley & Sons, NY, 1996.

Roberts, J.M., *A Short History of the World*, Oxford University Press, Oxford, 1993.

Rose, Mark, "Celebrating an Island Heritage," *Archaeology*, July-August, 1997.

Santillana, Giorgio de, and Dechend, Hertha von, *Hamlet's Mill*, Gambit Inc, Boston, 1969.

Sesti, Giuseppe Maria, *The Glorious Constellations*, Harry N Abrams, Inc., NY, 1987.

Silberman, Neil Asher, "The World of Paul," *Archaeology*, November-December 1997.

Soustell, Jacques, *The Olmecs*, Doubleday & Co., NY, 1984.

Stover, Leon E, and Kraig, Bruce, *Stonehenge, the Indo-European Heritage*, Nelson-Hall, Chicago, 1978.

Sullivan, William, *The Secret of the Incas*, Crown Publishers Inc, NY, 1996.

Tirion & Crossen, *Binocular Astronomy*, Willman-Bell Inc., Richmond, VA, 1992.

Ulansey, David, *The Origins of the Mithraic Mysteries*, Oxford University Press, NY, 1989.

Velikovsky, Immanuel, *Worlds in Collision*, The Macmillan Co, NY, 1950.

Ibid., *Ages in Chaos*, Doubleday & Co, NY, 1952.

Ibid., *Earth in Upheaval*, Doubleday & Co, NY, 1955.

Ibid., *Ramses II and his Time*, Doubleday & Co, NY, 1978.

Ibid., *Stargazers and Grave Diggers*, William Morrow & Co, 1983 .

Wenke, Robert J., *Patterns in Prehistory*, Oxford University Press, Oxford, 1984.

Willetts, R. F., *The Civilization of Ancient Crete*, Barnes & Noble, NY, 1995.

Woolley, Sir Leonard, *A Forgotten Kingdom*, Penguin Books, Baltimore, MD, 1953.

Maria Kay Simms

The New Age, Aquarius and Millennium Myths

What does the term "New Age" mean, anyway? A hodgepodge concept of every fringe element movement that is out of the mainstream and therefore suspicious and possibly subversive? A religion? A marketing ploy? A reemergence of the Goddess? The fabled "Age of Aquarius" popularized through the 1960s-revolution musical hit, *Hair*? A major "paradigm shift"[1] of such importance that it will transform our culture into a Utopian ideal of peace, prosperity, equality and higher consciousness? What you think, among that wide ranging group of possibilities, or any others you might name, is largely a matter of perspective. Whatever you think, you probably, to some extent, associate the term with the coming of the 21st century. Whatever you think, it's probably somewhat of a misconception. From what I read and see around me, I think it would be fair to say "none of the above," and at the same time, "all of the above." Whatever you or I think it is, each one of the above

---

[1] "Paradigm shift" is a term that has become overused to the point of cliche, but it is a convenient one to describe a change in consciousness that has been going on for quite some time. In the past few years, it has branched out of the fringe movements to at least begin to get the attention of the masses. A "paradigm" is defined by the older version of Webster's Dictionary that I happen to have immediately at hand as "an outstandingly clear or typical example of archetype." I wouldn't be surprised if newer versions of the dictionary also define it as "a model," because that is how I've heard it described many times. (Dictionaries, like history books, get rewritten as mass thinking changes.) In any case, "paradigm shift" refers to a change (shift) in the way the masses think—in the core concepts that are so basic most people just take them for granted, and build many other assumptions upon them.

represents reality—the Truth—for some people. For others, none of the above will quite fit. That's OK. I respect and honor diversity of opinion, and the fact that we are free to express it is one of the primary reasons I am so glad to have been born and raised in this country.

Since you are reading this book, it's fair for me to assume that you are interested in my opinion of what this New Age/ Millennium is all about. I'm one of those who think it's "none of the above." I think that a great deal of what is being expressed about the New Age from, let's say "outsiders," as well as how it is understood by many "insiders," overlooks a very significant point, that in my opinion, is at the core of the paradigm shift that is occurring.

Whatever we might say about the major changes that are occurring in this century—the technological explosion, the information explosion—I think that at the very core is a redefinition of how we view God (however one may define He, She or It) and ourselves in relation to God. Of this you may be saying, "this is nothing new," and on the surface, I would agree. Many have already written about the current expressions of spiritual hunger arising out of a culture that has become too materialistic and lost its spiritual center. Especially in this past year or two, major magazines and newspapers have featured various aspects of a massive search for meaning and hope. We are seeing revivals in established religions and a whole myriad of alternative spiritualities, as well as what has been called "a supermarket approach" to religion, as seekers pick and choose what to believe or not believe from a variety of philosophies. Astrologers are not surprised at this recent increase. We see it as a reflection of Pluto (which symbolizes slow, massive upheaval, transformation and rebirth) moving through Sagittarius (the zodiac sign most associated with religion, law, education and higher philosophy). A Pluto transit through a sign, however, is only a wink in time compared to the 2000+ years transit of a Great Age of the Zodiac.

The redefinition of God and so-called paradigm shift to which I am referring is a much more massive change than can be read into one generation or attributed to either a Pluto transit or the onset of the 21st century. The core issue of that redefinition is not so much a matter of **who** God is, but **where** God is. This is the point that is being overlooked in reams of material that are being written about the coming Millennium and all the various spiritual quests that are a part of it.

Where is God? Even I did not consciously deal with that issue as a main theme in my first book, *Twelve Wings of the Eagle*. In that book I correlated the symbolism of the Great Ages of the Zodiac with religious history, scripture and symbols, showing how God concepts, and consequent cultural changes have shifted with the ages. I linked the reemergence of deity as Goddess as an inevitable major trend, along with the redefining of the female/male roles, as we moved toward the final stage of the Age of Pisces. I predicted that by the onset of the Age of Aquarius, Goddess as a personification of deity would be in general acceptance within the collective consciousness.

When I wrote "Twelve Wings," in 1981-82, I was coming primarily from a Christian perspective. I was still active in the Catholic Church, even teaching confirmation catechism in my local parish. I was reading about the emerging Goddess movement in feminist spirituality, and was attracted by it, but had not yet acted on my inner feeling of rightness about it. Years later, after I had left the church, and begun studying with a Wiccan circle, I reread my own book, which was at long last being published. It was only then that I fully realized I had defined core concepts very central to the reasons why discovering Neo-Pagan spirituality, was for me, like "coming home." Even more basic to my analysis of the latter centuries of the Age of Pisces as a return of the Goddess, I had proposed a shift from linear to cyclical thinking, and I defined God as being within—immanent within all living things—rather than "out there," separate and above the physical universe. I said:

> Although in the material universe...most orbits are imperfect (elliptical), still all goes "round and round" in endless circuits. Perhaps through the symbol of the circle we can imagine...a dimension of one wholeness where no separate parts exist in separate spaces from each other. Is this the Oneness in Being that we call God?
>
> In Christianity we say Christ is "one in being with the Father." This is the meaning of the Ascension. Perhaps where many of us fall

short of full understanding of the Ascension is that we perceive Christ-one-with-the-Father as being out there, always and forever separated from our own potential...even in our imagination of Paradise. As a natural consequence of our linear thinking, the principle of opposites must take effect. God must have an opposite, and so we imagine a Satan that is also "out there"...Satan can only exist in the perception of separation from unity. If we perceive ourselves as one with God, if we bring God into the center of our being...then we must perceive that all souls are one with God. We have eliminated the line of polarity and have become the One, the center of the circle. We have found our soul, and we realize that the responsibility for our perception of the universe rests within. We are the creators of our reality, and the extent to which we hold ourselves in separation is a matter of personal choice.

When we think in circles instead of lines, we also neatly eliminate any "end time." Perceived endings are only change. The wheel is ever-turning, the cycle begins again—a new beginning, hopefully with growth based on experience.

In no way am I saying that either linear or cyclical, or God within or "out there" concepts are exclusive to Christianity, Paganism, the New Age, or any other defined movement or sect. In "Twelve Wings" I wrote about them from a Christian perspective; in a more recent book, *The Witch's Circle*, I wrote about them from a Pagan perspective. There are some individuals and movements within all such groups emphasizing an inner, personal connection with deity, and there are others who hold "out there" God/Satan dualistic, linear concepts. To make the cultural impact of where one stands on this issue a bit clearer, let's rephrase the issue of "where is God?" to "where is the Power?" An outgrowth of how the mainstream determines the answers to those questions has ramifications that permeate every aspect of our social/political structure.

The paradigm of God Within is struggling to emerge in the face of great conflict from the old paradigm of God "out there." On a bit less esoteric level, this addresses whether we, as a collective culture, will continue to project our power outside ourselves, or recognize that it dwells within, along with all the personal responsibility that goes with it. Shall we be victims, powerless in the face of overwhelming social problems, longing for Jesus, guardian angels, the planets, aliens, or more mundanely, the government, our lawyer, our boss, the leader of our particular religious sect, our psychic or astrologer, to set things right? Or shall we realize our own divinity and our connection with all that is! With that realization, we accept or reject the opinions of others according to our own higher consciousness, and then accept our own individual personal right, power and responsibility to create a better world.

In this reprise of "Twelve Wings" that I've been asked to write for this Millennium book, I will select a few excerpts that give you background for understanding how changing concepts of God have reflected the change in ages of the zodiac, as defined by the precession of the equinoxes. I'll use the symbolism of the signs of the zodiac to project how the future of this Age of Pisces may unfold, and what might be expected when we finally do get to the Age of Aquarius.

When we *finally* get there? Yes, I think the Age of Aquarius is far, far into the future. Not even our great-great-great grandchildren will see it. Yes, I am aware that other astrologers have written elaborate correlations of Aquarian symbolism with current trends in order to establish that we are in the Age of Aquarius or almost there. I don't agree, and one of the main thrusts of this article will be to tell you why.

My opinions stem from a study of the precession of the equinoxes that is the technical basis for determining the cycle of the Great Ages of the Zodiac. This puts us most definitely in the Age of Pisces for hundreds of years to come. Not coincidentally, it is very easy to describe cultural trends in terms of this symbolism. Of the fact that one can also find trends to reflect other signs, I can say only this: just as it is possible (and often happens) that one can extract a verse from the *Bible* to justify just about any position you want to take, it is also possible to apply astrological symbolism to rationalize just about anything you want to believe. That does not mean the *Bible* is wrong, and it most certainly does not invalidate astrology, any more than science is invalidated by the fact that statistical proof has sometimes been found to justify assumptions that are later proven to be erroneous.

I offer this description of our age, and our future, in terms of the Pisces archetype not just because it technically fits with precession, but because its watery, feminine, mystical/visionary symbology fits much better with the concept of Universal Love. This is the core concept that we, as a species, need to assimilate before we are ready to cope with the airy, intellectual Aquarian paradigm that will seek to discover Universal Truth.

As background for those readers who are new to astrology, I'll begin by excerpting the "Twelve Wings" interpretations of the basic nature of each astrological sign. References to how signs are reflected in cultural trends are just variations on the same themes that would apply to the signs as reflections of individual expression.

Understanding Basic Astrological Sign Symbolism

The signs of the zodiac, in the traditional order of the seasons, beginning with spring equinox, are:

Aries the Ram bends his horns and thrusts forward assertively and often impulsively. Dynamic, forceful and pioneering, Aries is quick to take the initiative on a new project, but leaves to others the tedium of follow-through. Aries is active, energetic, ardent, spontaneous and thinks "me first"...The Aries impulse to be always first is strong in initiative and courageous leadership—or it is headstrong selfishness that demands its own way.

Taurus the Bull has the settled persistence to structure and build upon the projects that Arian types have begun. The expertise of Taurus is reflected in the term, "bull market," which denotes prosperous growth. Taurus is materialistic, sensual, possessive, stubborn, patient and loves to be comfortable...Taurus stubbornness gives the perseverance to achieve mastery—or obstinate resistance to necessary change.

Gemini the Twins. As the twins are two, so is duality the nature of Gemini. Mentally quick and restless, two sides are seen to every question; two paths to every destination. Gemini is versatile, flexible, articulate, inquisitive and loves to communicate...Gemini's duality is versatile and adaptable, able to see new possibilities in a situation, from different points of view—or duality can also mean scattered, fickle irresponsibility.

Cancer the Crab is soft and sensitive inside, but is surrounded by a hard, protective shell. The "shel-ter" is home, and home and family are the vital interests. Cancer is emotional, motherly, nurturing, sentimental and remembers everything...The Cancer's maternal instincts are nurturing and caring, warm and protective—or possessive, anxious and smothering.

Leo the Lion radiates royal authority and self-confidentially expects the spotlight of center stage. Leo is proud, outgoing, demonstrative, generous, grandiose, dominating and dramatic...Leo's confidence radiates warmth, strength and generosity—or domineering authority and pomposity.

Virgo the Virgin, who carries a sheaf of wheat, separates the wheat from the chaff. She skillfully attends to the practical details of daily living. Virgo is discriminating, productive, efficient, critical, analytical, discreet, modest and loves to serve...Virgo's ability to discriminate is highly ethical and very efficient—or narrow-minded, petty and nit-picking.

Libra the Balance weighs and considers and compromises in order that peace and harmony can prevail. Libra, the symbol of partnership, is cooperative, fair and deeply appreciative of beauty...Libra compromise keeps the peace with tact, diplomacy, moderation and balance—or anxiously vacillates in a constant search for approval.

Scorpio the Scorpion has a deadly sting, which more often than not, is turned on self. Complex, passionate and intense, the Scorpion can live in the lower nature, coarse, sensual and sarcastic; or can rise to fly as the Eagle, to share strength with brilliant magnetism. The symbol of degeneration and regeneration, death and rebirth, Scorpio is penetrating, secretive and very strong willed... Scorpio's power to control can be turned inward for self-discipline and revitalizing strength—or outward, to manipulate others.

Sagittarius the Archer enthusiastically shoots arrows of ideas into everyone he meets. With fervent idealism, he shoots his arrows for the highest stars. Sometimes the goal-oriented Archer will focus his enthusiasm on competitive sports or travel, as well as on ideas. Sagittarius is optimistic, truthful, tactless and adventurous... Sagittarius enthusiastically inspires others with idealism—or dogmatically insists what everyone must believe.

Capricorn the Goat ambitiously climbs to the top of the mountain. Coolly pragmatic, responsible and organized, she will become the executive or the tyrant of her particular mountain. Capricorn is cautious, conservative, serious, dutiful and status-seeking... Capricorn's ability to concentrate on reality is responsible, practical and just—or opportunistic and unscrupulous.

Aquarius the Waterbearer pours out the contents of his urn to benefit the masses. Universalistic and humanitarian, he rebels against any elitist figure of authority. Friend of everyone, yet emotionally detached, he is often misunderstood by those who would like to be close to him. Aquarius is individualistic, independent and non-conforming...Aquarius nonconformity can be the humanitarian who strives for needed reform in society—or the radical who rebels against everything that restricts personal freedom.

Pisces the Fishes is two fishes, tied together, but swimming in opposite directions. Contradictory in nature, the Pisces often seems to work against herself. Yet at her best, she has an intuitive sense of the synthesis of all contradictions. Sympathetic and compassionate, Pisces can be the savior or the victim. Pisces is imaginative, often psychic, impressionable and self-sacrificing...Self-sacrificing Pisces serves with loving compassion and great empathy—or wallows in the self-pity of the suffering martyr.

Each sign is said to have its complementary opposite, the sign that lies directly across the diameter of the zodiac circle. Each pair of opposite signs share with each other two basic qualities. They are both either cardinal, fixed or mutable. They are both either positive or negative. Even more importantly it must be understood that complementary opposites are really like two sides of one coin. Since each emphasizes character traits that tend to be weak and undeveloped in their opposite sign, conflict may be perceived. Actually they are like two halves of a whole. In order to achieve wholeness it is especially necessary to understand and integrate the opposition.

One of the themes to understand in my application of astrological symbolism to the Great Ages is the interplay of opposition signs. The sign of the age is portrayed as the ideal, or the collective concept of deity. Humanity, itself, is symbolized by the opposite sign. If God is perceived as the epitome of the virtues of the sign of the age, then not-God (humanity), at its collective best and worst, epitomizes the sign of opposition. We mortals must strive for understanding of and integration with our God in order to become "holy" (whole).

As a brief example of the complementary opposites, the following section gives one of the primary issues common to each pair, and the contrasting manner in which each deals with that issue.

Aries opposite Libra: IDENTITY

Aries asserts self, while Libra seeks self-identity through relating to others.

Taurus opposite Scorpio: MASTERY

Taurus finds security in mastery of the material world. Scorpio finds power through mastery of the inner self.

Gemini opposite Sagittarius: WISDOM

Gemini sees truth through reason and logic. Sagittarius sees truth through revelation and faith.

Cancer opposite Capricorn: COMMUNITY

Cancer protects and nurtures the home and family life. Capricorn advances and protects the professional and public life.

Leo opposite Aquarius: LEADERSHIP

Magnanimously and generously, Leo rules. Egalitarian Aquarius rebels against the rule of any individual.

Virgo opposite Pisces: SERVICE

Virgo, the realist, is unselfishly dedicated to fulfill earthly human needs. Pisces, the visionary, is selflessly devoted to the needs of the spirit.

The signs, as presented here, are only a small part of the complex language of astrology. Each individual person can be described according to a unique composite of all signs. All twelve appear somewhere among the planets and houses of every horoscope. The interpretation of a horoscope must be further clarified within the context of the individual's particular heredity and environment.

Regardless of their individual horoscopes, however, all people are influenced by the collective world view of the time in which they live, even though they may be totally unconscious of that fact. A paradigm defined by a slow-moving precessional age spans many generations and links diverse peoples and cultures throughout the world. Most people are totally unaware of the synchronicity between the symbolism of the precessional ages and the collective unconscious. Yet religion, structured through the projection of that collective unconscious, bears striking correspondence with the astrological sign of each precessional age.

For two thousand years Aries has been called the first sign of the zodiac. The point of the vernal equinox, first day of spring, when the Sun, apparently (from the viewpoint of Earth) moves northward across the Great Circle in space scribed by Earth's equator, is called the zero degree of Aries, the beginning of the 360° zodiacal circle.[2]

---

[2] The word zodiac may refer to any of several systems of dividing the ecliptic. The **constellational zodiac** maps the actual constellations that lie beyond the path of the ecliptic. They are very unequal in size in terms of the number of degrees that would be alloted to each ecliptical sector. Some overlap and there are gaps into which non-zodiac constellations intrude. The **tropical zodiac** is an equal division measurement of the ecliptic, alloting 30° to each sign, beginning with the point of the vernal equinox. This zodiac clearly defines the seasons, drives much of its symbolism from the seasons, and

continued on next page

The signs of the equinoxes and solstices are called, in astrological language, the **cardinal signs**. Cardinal means that which is of prime importance, upon which other things hinge. **The cardinal signs symbolize the acting, creating, initiating quality of life.**

Aries was not always the first sign. In the Age of Aries the zodiac was led by Aldebaran, the "bull's eye" of Taurus. Taurus, Leo, Scorpio and Aquarius were called the four corners of the world, or the Guardians, in the ancient mysteries. The change of the ages was marked by Aries the Ram, with Cancer, Libra and Capricorn becoming the new cardinal points. **Aries, the cardinal ascendant, is the most direct expression of the action principle in this Age of Pisces.**

The cardinal signs are one of three ways of grouping zodiac signs according to a quality or mode of expression. The other two groups are called fixed and mutable.

The **fixed signs** represent stability. Their quality is sustaining, durable and everlasting. Taurus, Leo, Scorpio and Aquarius are the fixed signs of this Age of Pisces. Long have these symbols been "fixed" in our collective consciousness, whether or not we consciously connect them with astrology. They are reflected in the biblical prophecies of Revelations and Ezekiel, involving the four "living creatures." They are found as parts of the sphinx in Egyptian art, and have also been associated with each Gospel in Christian art: Luke is Taurus, Mark is Leo, John is Scorpio and Matthew is Aquarius. Back nearly to the dawn of our recorded history bulls and cattle have been used as sacred symbols through much of the civilized world.

The **mutable signs**, in this age, are Gemini, Virgo, Sagittarius and Pisces. As the cardinal signs are initiating, the fixed sustaining, the mutable are disseminating. Adaptable and flexible in their expression, the mutable signs "spread the word" and disseminate knowledge.

---

continued from previous page
it is the one most widely used in western astrology. This is the zodiac that people are generally referring to when they ask "what's your sign" (even if they mistakenly think they are talking about a constellation!). The **sidereal zodiac** moves the vernal point in an attempt to keep the signs more in sync with the constellations. Still, the ecliptic is measured in equal 30° sectors, so they can't really match the unequal constellations, no matter which fixed star they choose to reference the zero point. There are actually multiple sidereal systems due to disagreement over exactly where that beginning point should be. Astronomers (who should know better) like to gibe astrology by saying we don't know where are signs really are. For shame!

Pisces is the constellation that rises just before the sun at vernal equinox. It is the constellation in this position that determines the archetype for the age. Pisces is a mutable sign. As the primary symbol of the changing order, Pisces must disseminate the truth and spread the word of the ideals of the new order.

Ideals may be wonderful, however actions are often based on past programming. So, a new concept, symbolized by the mutable sign of the New Age, is introduced, but the action decided upon to disseminate the new ideal is grounded in the habits of thinking that are the deeply entrenched and taken-for-granted concepts of the outgoing age. Understandably, a great deal of struggle and conflict takes place as human attempts to understand and to teach the ideals of the New Age are carried out with actions influenced by unconscious motivations carried over from the old paradigm!

In case you didn't notice just how difficult the reconciliation of old and new can be, read again the short individual sign interpretations. Notice how very different each sign is from the one next to it. There are no more abrasive mixes of archetypes in the zodiac than those that exist between adjacent signs.

The Precessional Ages

While viewing cultural evolution in terms of precessional ages, encompassing thousands of years, may seem way too broad in defining the approach of this Millennium, I urge you to consider it. The onset of the 21st century is being widely viewed with both fears of catastrophe and wild hopes that exceed reasonable expectation. Let's put it within the context of a larger perspective, to see what light can be shed on just where we (collectively) have been and where we are heading.

It seems to be human nature to want the most momentous events in history to happen within one's own lifetime, hence the frequency of Second Coming predictions. It's the wish for Utopia—to live for the time when something will happen to sweep away all the evils and pains of society and replace them with all that one perceives as good. The Age of Aquarius is a New Age version, touted in the song from the 60s musical hit, *Hair*, as the golden age "when the Moon is in the 7th house, and Jupiter aligns with Mars, then peace will guide the planets and love will steer the stars." Just as with the various prophecies of the time of Christ's return, the onset of the Age of Aquarius seems to depend on the expected lifetime of the prophet. When I was researching "Twelve Wings," I found psychic predictions written in the 30s that placed the Age of Aquarius as starting in the 50s, and so on forward, with every author putting the onset of Aquarius no more than 20 years hence. In current publications you can read that it's already here, or if not, it's surely due no more than 10 or 20 years into the 21st century.

The song from "Hair" was right in that the term "New Age" was originally coined to refer to the precessional ages of the zodiac, and the coming of the next Age of Aquarius. When it begins is an issue of far less agreement. A few astrologers have rationalized forms of measurement that will allow them to illustrate how we are "in" the Age of Aquarius, or at least "almost" in it. Others, who technically know better, have moved to a consideration of ancient astronomies such as the Mayan in order to find a rationale for a timing of the ages that would more closely coincide with the beginning of the 21st century. The following excerpt from *Twelve Wings of the Eagle*, explains what a precessional age is, and how I arrived at its timing:

> ...Although the stars in any given constellation are hundreds of light years away from each other, and at greatly varied distances from earth, to us they seem to be in family groups...The closest star to earth is, of course, the sun. The time that it takes for the earth to orbit the sun is how we determine our calendar year. As the earth circles the sun, it appears from earth that the sun is "in" (in front of) each of the twelve constellations of the zodiac in succession.... if you were able to look right at the sun at exactly the same time every day, it would appear to move steadily counter-clockwise, from west to east, as seen against the zodiac constellations. Since the sun is so bright, it overwhelms the stars—you can not see the constellations when the sun is out. But if you look at the night sky and follow the movement of a planet, like Mars, every night at the same time, you can see this motion.
>
> All of the planets in our solar system appear to us to move in the same plane as the sun does. This apparent path of the sun, which is actually the orbit of the earth around the sun, is known as the ecliptic. The zodiac is the group of constellations that can be seen right along the ecliptic.

A very important measurement used by astronomers and astrologers is the point of the vernal equinox. This is the point at which the sun appears to cross the plane of the earth's equator going northward on the first day of spring. It is a point of intersection of the circle, or plane, of the ecliptic ... and the circle, or plane, of the equator...

The earth is not a perfect sphere. It is slightly flat at the north and south poles and it bulges around the middle. Because of this, its spin on its axis is slightly irregular, much like the spin of a top that is just beginning to slow down.

If you play with a child's top for a while, you can begin to understand precession. Watch the tip ends. The tip that touches the floor seems stationary, but the top tip describes a circle. Then study the center. It wobbles a little.

The earth, in a similar way to the top, wobbles a little. To us, here on our wobbly planet, it looks like the intersections of equator and ecliptic are moving slowly clockwise along the path of the ecliptic.[3] This movement is extremely slow. It takes the vernal point almost 26,000 years to "wobble" past all the constellations of the zodiac, completing an entire circuit of the ecliptic. [This is the phenomenon known as the precession of the equinoxes.]

...How did the ancients figure this out? Their priests studied the sky very carefully night after night. Many things depended on the accuracy of their observations—success of the planting seasons, and therefore the livelihood of the people; religion, and the power, or perhaps the very lives of the priests. Among the more careful observations were of the equinoctial and solstice points.

If over the years you noticed that a certain star that you expected to rise heliacally (meaning just before the sun) on the first day of spring, was no longer visible, you could make the assumption that something up there had shifted. Now assuming you are well aware of the twelve constellations along the ecliptic; you now see that only one star of a given constellation is still visible just before sunrise. You would know that in a few years that one, too, would be invisible, and the next constellation in line would rise before the sun. The entire constellation that had risen heliacally for as long as you or anyone else you knew could remember would then be completely invisible (lost in the blinding rays of the sun.) What would you make of that?

The ancients decided that a whole new order had arrived. The constellation that now rose right with the sun, and was thus invisible, was said to be "sacrificed".[4] At the dawn of the Age of Aries, one

---

[3] The comparison of precession to a child's top is from *Stars and Men* by Stephen and Margaret Ionides, Indianapolis and New York, Bobbs-Merrill Co., 1939.

[4] The explanation of how the ancients observed the coming of a new age is from *Hamlet's Mill* by Giorgio de Santillana and Hertha von Dechend, Boston, Gambit, Inc., 1969.

of the most popular animals to be offered on the sacrificial altars was the bull or calf, symbol of the "sacrificed" Age of Taurus. The symbol of the Ages of Aries was the Ram, and ram or fire deities quickly began to compete with the bull-gods and sacred cows for the devotion of the people. As the new order became more firmly established, those who slipped back into the old ways worshipped a watered-down version of the bull, a little bull—the golden calf.

By the end of the Age of Aries, the ram had become a lamb; and as Aries became lost, or sacrificed, in the sunrise and the Age of Pisces dawned, the Christ was understood to be the sacrificial lamb—the Lamb of God who gave his own life for the redemption of humanity

Now just before the Age of Pisces began, a Greek astronomer named Hipparchus studied precession. At that time, the constellation Aries no longer rose before the sun. Perhaps only the first star in the Ram could be seen at vernal equinox, and then, one year, it was invisible. Precessional order is said to be "backwards" so it is the "head" of the constellation that is the last to disappear at the horizon.

Hipparchus and others decided to call the point of the vernal equinox "the first point of Aries." The constellations are irregular in size, so for convenience of measurement of the celestial bodies, the circle of the ecliptic was divided into twelve equal sections of 30 degrees each. The sections were named according to the constellations that appeared approximately within them, and the degrees were numbered in counter-clockwise order according to the sun's apparent yearly transit.

The equal sections of the ecliptic are what we call the signs of the zodiac. At the time of Hipparchus the signs and the constellations coincided with each other. Because of the precession of the equinox, this is no longer true. On the first day of spring it is now about the fourth degree from the beginning of the constellation Pisces that rises just before the sun. In a few hundred years, Pisces will have completely "disappeared," the constellation Aquarius will rise before the sun, and we will truly be in the Age of Aquarius.

On the timing of the Great Ages there is little agreement. Most books on the subject advocate an equal division of the approximately 26,000 year long Great Year cycle into 2000 to 2200 year long Great Months, or Ages. Nearly every author agrees that Jesus brought in the Age of Pisces the Fishes. As the "sacrificial lamb" of the outgoing age, he founded a new religion with disciples who were "fishers of men" and followers who recognized each other by the sign of the fish.

My initial dissatisfaction with equal division measurement was because history just didn't fit. I could find no significant Aries symbolism for 2000 years before Christ. Not until after 1800 BC does Ram symbolism become prominent. Why?

As I looked at a star map, the answer became clear. The constellations are not the same size, so how could the ages be the same length? Aries is tiny, compared to Pisces. It would take hundreds of years longer for the equinox to precess through the Fishes than through the Ram!

I searched in vain for a reference that would tell me exactly how many degrees were in each constellation. Astronomers' star maps usually indicate only each 15th degree of the ecliptic. I learned that even though the stars are apparently fixed in position, they do move in space enough that new star maps are prepared at fifty to one hundred year intervals. Although the "proper" motion is extremely slow, it obviously would be enough to change the size and shape of constellations slightly over a period of several thousand years.

It would seem that the only way to know exactly when the last star of a constellation rose just before the sun on the day of the vernal equinox, heralding the end of an Age, would be to be there— or to have access to a star chart drawn at that time.

Another obstacle to the exact timing of ages is that the rate of precession is slightly accelerating. The mean length of a Great Year is at present 25,920 years.

Finally, I found a list of degrees for unequal sections of the ecliptic, set up by astronomers for the purpose of locating stars. Compared with the star maps, the list matched the constellations, if the degrees of the "open spaces" between some of the constellations are added to the nearest small one.

(I place "open" in quotes because obviously the spaces are not open. In fact, at least two non-zodiacal constellations appear to intrude within the degree spread assigned to the ecliptic. However all of the astronomy texts seemed to be comfortably in agreement that there are twelve zodiac constellations. Apparently the historical and symbolic significance of twelve is acceptable as a precedent to astronomers, so I will not complicate my theory by speculating on the meaning of Ophichus or Cetus.)

At any rate, I decided to use the astronomers' list to work a ratio to a total Great Year cycle of 25,920 years, just to see if the results worked better with past historical evidence. To do this I divided the degrees of a full circle, 360, by the number of degrees for each constellation. The result was then divided into 25,920...

In the light of the facts of acceleration of precession and proper motion of the stars, and of the controversy over the actual beginning of the Piscean Age, it makes no sense to try to pinpoint an exact year, or even an exact decade for the division between epochs. A transition period of at the very least, one hundred years, would have to be considered at each division, with an even larger transition period at the divisions between which there are several degrees of "open" space: Leo/Cancer, Gemini/Taurus, Pisces/Aquarius, and Capricorn/Sagittarius. Therefore, it seemed only reasonable to round off my figures to the nearest hundred years, and to add or subtract from zero, which may not be exactly the year of the birth of Christ, but is close, and is commonly accepted as the one upon which the calendar is based.

According to the above reasoning, my estimate of the approximate length of each age, and its beginning (preceding or following the current age) is as follows:

Constellation	Degrees	Years in Age	Beginning Year
Libra	18	1296	15,000 BC
Virgo	46	3312	13,600 BC
Leo	35	2521	10,000 BC
Cancer	21	1512	7,800 BC
Gemini	28	2016	6,300 BC
Taurus	36	2592	4,300 BC
Aries	24	1728	1,700 BC
Pisces	38	2737	AD 1
Aquarius	25	1800	AD 2,700
Capricorn	28	2016	AD 4,500
Sagittarius	30	2160	AD 6,500
Scorpio	31	2232	AD 8,600

I began with Libra as the sign of balance, and correlated it to the biblical Eden, as the beginning of the current Great Year. Scorpio, as the sign of death/rebirth was the end of the Great Year and the beginning of a new one.

Later I found that astrologer Rob Hand had also been working with the constellational size idea for the ages. With a considerably more precise methodology than mine, using computer calculations and a star map of Ptolemy, Rob timed the precession of the vernal point past each individual star in the Pisces constellation, and correlated historical events to it. His very interesting study is published in his book *Essays on Astrology*, Rockport, MA: ParaResearch, 1982. Rob came up with 2813 A. D. as the time that the vernal point comes to Beta Piscium, the last star in the Pisces constellation. That would put his beginning of the Age of Aquarius even later than mine, by over 100 years.

So, if this New Age isn't Aquarius, and we are still in the Age of Pisces, what does that mean? In "Twelve Wings," I dubbed the trend I predicted to peak in the early decades of the 21st century as a "New Renaissance." I see it as, at long last, a time when the masses may truly adopt the paradigm introduced at the onset of the Age of Pisces, and actually **live** it, minus the conflicted habits of thinking that are a carryover from the previous Age of Aries. Old habits of thinking die very slowly, in the collective consciousness even more so than in individuals.

Pisces, the age we are "in" and have been in for around 2000 years, is a complex age that has seen three major paradigm shifts: the Age of Faith, the Renaissance, and the Age of Reason (also called Age of Enlightenment). All three of these, though, are subsidiary to the massive paradigm defined by the Piscean Age itself: the redefinition of God according to a basic symbolism that corresponds to a shift from Aries to Pisces.

Ages change very slowly, and the transition period from one to the next can take a very long time. The point to consider, in regard to a major paradigm shift, is at what point a new model or archetype becomes part of MASS consciousness. The "cutting edge" is always eons ahead of the masses. The cutting edge is often a predictor of trends, but it is not until a concept becomes so entrenched in the mass consciousness that it is taken for granted, that it then becomes the Truth upon which other assumptions are based. At that point the shift has faded into ancient history, and a new mass paradigm is firmly entrenched as the model to which a new cutting edge will then eventually emerge to rebel against.

The transition from the Age of Aries into the Age of Pisces was marked by a redefinition of God from the fiery and fearful patriarchal deity of Old Testament times to the compassionate, loving and forgiving paternal figure portrayed by Jesus. Although Jesus the Christ is heralded by many millions as the savior, God incarnate, he was not the only avatar whom we could associate with the Piscean paradigm. He is, however, the one most widely recognized in Western civilization, which has been the power center in this age. Because of the dominance of the west, our very system of dating time is based on the supposed year of his birth, however erroneously that year may have been originally set![5] Because my part of this book is supposed to be based on a recap of "Twelve Wings," most of my analysis of the Age of Pisces centers on Christianity.

First, though, I do want to emphasize that the Piscean ideals, the more compassionate, mystical vision of a deity of love, was introduced by other great teachers as well—the Buddha, Lao-tzu, Confucius, Msahvira, to name a few. Most pre-dated Jesus by a few hundred years, but all are within what could rightly be called a transition period from Aries to Pisces.

A study of the teachings of Siddhartha Gautama (c. 500 BC), who departed radically from Hinduism to found Buddhism, and became known as the Buddha, is a very important figure. His teachings, of all the others, could be said to have retained the purity of vision that is a reflection of Pisces throughout this age, with the least overlay of Arian patriarchal abuses. In further reflection of the most positive qualities of the flowering of the Piscean Age, Buddhism is enjoying a rapidly growing interest in the west, both for itself, and in various blendings with the also rapidly growing Neo-Pagan alternative spiritualities.

Here, then, is the past of the Age of Pisces, as it is reflected by the western cultures who have been dominated by the Christian concept of deity, and as it is excerpted from "Twelve Wings."

The Virgin, the Son and the Age of the Fishes

...The use of symbolism in the gospels certainly suggests that at least some early Christian writers and quite possibly Jesus, himself, were knowledgeable in astrology and in the ancient mystery religions. Yet contemporary church authorities ignore this quite com-

---

[5] Hundreds of years after the life of Jesus, the monk, Dionysius Exiguus the Less, who invented the B.C./A.D. method of counting years, quite simply, miscalculated. His choice for the first year just doesn't mesh with other facts, such as for example, that King Herod, who in the Gospels, was very much alive when Jesus was born, actually died in 4 B.C. Controversy abounds on just what year, by that system, Jesus was born, but the majority opinion among astrologers, astronomers and theologians seems to be 6 or 7 B.C. Another technicality pertinent to our understanding of the coming millennium is that Dionysius named his first year A.D. number **one**, which means that the year 2000 is the last year of the 20th century, not the first year of the 21st!

pletely in their explanations (or often lack of explanation) of the obviously symbolic passages. Why is this so? A brief historical sketch of the western culture where Christianity found its center will help explain.[6]

Nothing makes a group more united than outside persecution, so we can rightly assume a great spiritual closeness among the early Christians who hid in the catacombs and identified each other with the secret sign of the fish. They believed that Christ's promised second coming, and their own enraptured deliverance from this earth, was due at any moment, and that was all that really mattered to them.

But as the dangers of Roman persecution decreased, the disagreements among the faithful increased, and accusations of heresy abounded. Various factions wrangled over differing ideas of doctrine, each small community (church) supporting its opinion with this or that passage from the letters of St. Paul, and each labeling any dissenting person or church 'heretical.' The corrupted Aries attitudes of Old Testament time were far from overcome, despite the teachings of Jesus to the contrary. The symbol of the old age had become the 'rising sign,' the cardinal ascendant, of the new age. Jesus' teachings would be spread by men acting in the manner of Aries. Initiative in the new age was motivated by habit patterns carried over from old Arian concepts. Old patterns of thinking, like old ages, die very slowly. Heretics and unbelievers were to be stamped out, violently if necessary.

The second coming didn't come and the original apostles died out. New generations began to realize that Christians might have to live in the world for a long time, so some kind of authority to settle all the wrangling was obviously necessary. The theory was accepted that the apostles had appointed bishops to succeed them, and that only those in direct line of succession from the apostles could ordain new priests. As the bishops began to meet to regulate the affairs of the church, the wrangling over doctrine proceeded with greater order. One of the methods through which they sought to unite the many rather independent and loosely related churches was to begin to collect and select a group of definite Christian writings to form a New Testament. Soon, sometime in the 2nd century, the term 'Catholic' came into general use. The word means 'universal,' meaning 'all,' but in the actual fact of the matter, a better definition would be 'exclusive' or 'orthodox.' The strongest faction within the churches grew up in the capital city of Rome and the Bishop of Rome was proclaimed to be the direct successor of St. Peter and therefore the head of the church.

---

[6] Much of the information in this historical sketch is repeated in a number of sources I've read and can no longer identify. For more detail on church history, I recommend *The Great Religions*, Richard Cavendish, New York, Arco Publ., Inc., 1980; *Founded on a Rock*, Louis de Wohl, Philadelphia and New York, J.B. Lippincott, Co., 1961; and *The New Catholic Encyclopedia*, Catholic University of America, 1979.

With the recognition of Christianity by the Emperor Constantine in 313, persecution ceased, and the bishops found themselves to be quite powerful. Now disputes with the prevailing hierarchy could be put down with the help of the state.

One doctrinal dispute, for example, at the Church Council at Nicea in 325, centered around a priest named Arius, whose name bears an amusing similarity to the zodiac sign of Aries. I was amused by the name and by the dispute [which was called, no kidding, the Arian controversy—the ideas of Arius hark back to the absolute monotheism that characterized the ideal of the old Arian Age.] Arius argued that since the father (God) must have existed before the son (Christ), the son could not be eternal and the father's equal. The majority of the bishops thought that this could not be so because if Christ was not fully God, the salvation of the believers in him was not assured. Arius was declared a heretic and Emperor Constantine obligingly had him exiled. The Nicean Creed [for this new religion of the Age Piscean, which amusingly rhymes with Nicean] was adopted, stating that Christ is of 'one substance with the Father'...

At the risk of oversimplification of a complicated subject, much of the controversy with which the early church hierarchy dealt was with a variety of sects that could be loosely grouped under the term 'Gnostic.'

Gnosticism, derived from the Greek gnosis (to know), was a broad synthesis of ideas that included the ancient mystery religions and astrology, along with elements of Judaism, Greek philosophy, and old Iranian, Syrian and Egyptian religions. In general, the Gnostics held that salvation is accomplished not by the power of God nor by human faith alone, but by spiritual growth through esoteric knowledge. The Christ-redeemer had a central place, but it was to communicate or reveal to men the saving knowledge, rather than to actually be their salvation.[7]

Gnostic ideas and symbolism undoubtedly influenced some of the books that wound up in the New Testament, but Gnostic think-ing was increasingly suppressed as the church institution took hold. The official doctrine that prevailed was that Christ's sacrifice on the cross completely redeemed humanity and that salvation is a gift from God through faith in Christ that is conferred on the recipient regardless of any merit... The attitude of the early church hierarchy seemed to be that knowledge (gnosis) as the path toward truth (God) was unnecessary, if not outright evil; and that faith alone could bring salvation—and that is all that mattered. The proper attention of man should be on ascetic preparation for his reward in the hereafter. After all, they thought, why should one waste time on

---

[7] This definition of Gnosticism is from *The New Catholic Encyclopedia*. For further study I suggest *The Gnostic Religion* by Hans Jonas, Boston, Beacon Hill, 1979.

such material matters as science, when Christ was due to return at any moment and whisk the faithful off to Heaven and heap great tribulations on everyone else?

But then, one wonders if perhaps at least a few influential members of the hierarchy were not immune to the attitude that an emphasis on faith alone, and a suppression of free inquiry, gave them much better control over the masses. The spectacular book-burning of the great Library of Alexandria in the 5th century so thoroughly contributed to such suppression, that by 1633 the Christian world was still ignorant of the knowledge about the cosmos that had been known to the classical Greeks. Galileo was condemned before the Catholic Inquisition for the 'heresy' of insisting that the earth was not the center of the universe, but instead was only one of a group of planets orbiting the sun. One of the books known to have been burned at Alexandria contained just that very concept for which Galileo was persecuted. It was written by Aristarchus at least 200 years before the birth of Christ.

...When Christianity became the official religion of the Roman Empire, great masses of people were instant converts. Careful preparation was no longer necessary for protection, and the numbers were overwhelming. The new Christians brought with them a background of worship of a wide variety of gods and goddesses, of rituals and of superstitions. The leaders of the young Christian church had a job on their hands of mammoth proportions.

... now, in the dark ages of the Age of Pisces, astrology [along with the other sciences] faded into obscurity ... deemed unnecessary to the total emphasis on faith that was the ideal of the new order.

This was the first major paradigm of the Age of Pisces, known in history books as the Age of Faith. With the overlay of Arian patriarchal attitudes, that faith was spread through often brutal conquest in the Crusades. From this extreme emphasis on faith, an opposite reaction would begin to emerge. I illustrated it with a pendulum, using the astrological signs in direct opposition and square to Pisces forming a:

... cross of matter that is also the major Christian symbol. At the top of our cross is our visionary ideal of Pisces—a compassionate, loving, forgiving concept of God that encompasses all people everywhere with love and faith in life eternal. At the opposite end of that pole, at the bottom, we are anchored in the down-to-earth reality of Virgo. We are at the moment still very much mortal, bound to material affairs, and must be concerned with what is useful, practical, and realistically within our grasp. It is from our reality of Virgo that we must reach out for our ideal vision in Pisces.

Just as Jesus on the cross had two insurgents, one to the left and one to the right; we humans, symbolically impaled on our cross of matter, have two symbols in square (conflict) with our central pole. With these we must contend as well, as we attempt to balance our vision with our reality.

One of the insurgents is said to have expressed faith in Jesus and was promised paradise. When 'one of the twelve, Thomas (the name means Twin)', insisted on reasonable proof of Jesus' resurrection, and was allowed to probe the wounds, Jesus said:

You became a believer because you saw me.

Blessed are they who have not seen and have believed.

John 20:24-29[8]

"The pendulum began its swing at the point of Sagittarius, faith in Revelation. At the opposite end of that pole is the 'twin'—Gemini, symbolizing Reason.[9]

The early church leaders (who as all mortals in this age are symbolized by the opposition sign of Virgo) were concerned with how to put the mystical Piscean vision of Jesus into a framework of

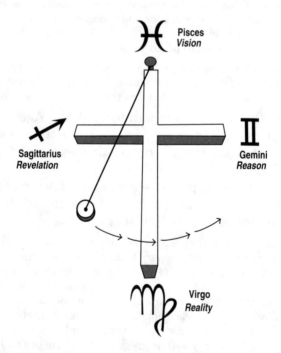

Pisces
Vision

Sagittarius
Revelation

Gemini
Reason

Virgo
Reality

---

[8] *New American Bible*, Catholic Version, Nashville, Camden, New York: Thomas Nelson Pub., 1971.

[9] Key words for Sagittarius and Gemini are the same as those used by Marcia Moore and Mark Douglas in *Astrology: A Divine Science*, York Harbor, Maine: Arcane Publications, 1971.

practical reality. They began with a typically Sagittarian dogmatic insistence on blind faith in a collected group of principles that they believed had been revealed to them through the Christ. No word in the gospels even implies that Jesus condemned the doubting Thomas. But Virgo is very discriminating, and in the discernment of the Virgoan Church, the attitude of Thomas met with grave disapproval. It was infinitely more blessed to believe what one was told to believe than to doubt and question and reason why.

As the symbolic pendulum swings out of the Age of Faith and passes center, we come to what could be called the mid-life crisis of our Piscean Age. It was a Renaissance of learning, but...

The individual discernment and the concepts of reality that did not fit into the official dogma had been too long suppressed. Like the 'shadow' of Carl Jung's psychology, it was about to erupt.[10] The pendulum would hit the pole of Reason with a vengeance.

In 1382, just about exactly half-way through the age, John Wyclif had produced the first English translation of the Bible, believing that common man should be able to read scripture for himself, rather than allow the Church, only, to interpret it for him. Wyclif was condemned as a heretic for his efforts, and his Bible was forbidden. But by the 15th and 16th centuries, the printing press had spread new translations of the Bible all over Europe and the Protestant Reformation was a reality.[11]

No longer could one church control what the people believed. By the time the Catholic Church tried to silence Galileo, the old dogmatic days were nearly over. Virgoan discrimination splintered Christianity into dozens of denominations, each bickering with the others over often minute details of difference in their interpretation of theology and scripture. Quite independently of the churches, great advances were being made in scientific observations; and there was a great revival of interest in all of the humanities and in long suppressed Greek classics.

As the pendulum swung out of the golden age of Renaissance, a dark age for matters of faith was about to emerge. The new paradigm came to be called the Age of Reason, and it reached its peak in the 18th century.

In the cross that all of collective humanity bears in this Piscean Age, religion tends to over-emphasize the poles of Pisces (Vision) and Sagittarius (Revelation); while science tends to over-emphasize the opposite poles of Virgo (Reality) and Gemini (Reason). ... in the

---

[10] My thoughts that correlate Jungian psychology to astrology were first influenced by Liz Green's *Relating*, Samuel Weiser, Inc. 1978.

[11] Readers Digest, *Atlas of the Bible*, Pleasantville, NY, 1981, pg. 26.

18th century, prevailing thought became dominated by materialistic science...The attention of nearly all the first-rate minds riveted on the material universe. The intellectual establishment discredited any assumptions about the nature of the universe that could not be supported by rigorous scientific investigation. Scientists had no time to consider unproved assumptions based on human experience or revelation. Interest in the intangible spirit waned to zero. Rationalism and materialism became the reigning philosophies.

...The church and its Biblical scholars... reeled under the on-slaught of materialistic science. Darwin's theory of evolution, for example, called to question the credibility of the Bible. Genesis had been considered to be literally accurate. If it was not, then in what way was it accurate? Over the years, the now weakened religious authorities had to readjust to the now dominant thought of Reason. The plain fact had to be accepted that scripture could be interpreted in more than one way.[12]

No longer did any one Christian denomination have the power to brutally persecute as heretics those who held dissenting views. Scholars sought ways to explain the *Bible* in a rational manner that would have at least some reasonable conformity to the 'proven' scientific facts that had won general acceptance.

... in this latter half of the 20th century, it has become quite noticeable that the pendulum is swinging toward center. No longer does pure reason dominate the accepted world view. Scientists—at least many of them—are admitting that accepted 'proven' scientific facts have been disproved—and each apparent solution only provokes another question. The study of human experience has returned to respectability as a proper subject for scientific investigation. Such intangibles as human intuition are taken seriously.

Along with the general revival of interest in humanism, astrology, too, has made a massive comeback in popularity. Many talented and well-educated people now consider astrology a worthy subject for serious investigation, and openly call themselves astrologers. Serious writing and research abounds.

... astrology at its highest level... can be a tool for the synthesis of science (Reason) and religion (Revelation); and synthesis of these two is inevitable and necessary...The quest for connective links and synthesis and a wholistic view must go on in all fields of study if we are to achieve the golden age of peace and tolerance and humanitarian concern that is our vision for the future. To be sure, these pages present only a small part of that synthesis. But each of us must reach out from where we are, in the hope that our thoughts may blend with others into a new level of understanding.

---

[12] Cavendish, *The Great Religions*

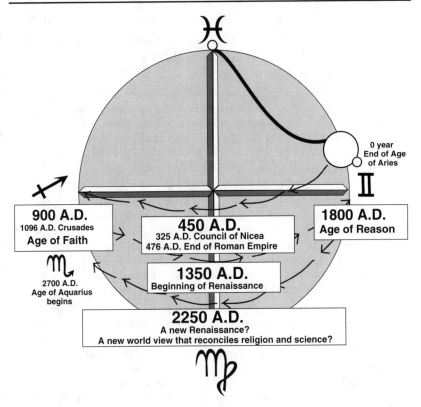

If, indeed, we are moving toward a "New Renaissance" when the two extremes of faith and reason will once again reach a balance point—when an overly materialistic world will have regained its spiritual center, in balance with an enlightened modern science—when will it be and how will it come about?

In dividing the Age of Pisces into thirds, as shown in the pendulum illustration, I placed the full flowering of this New Age—a new Renaissance (rebirth) of a "golden age"— at about AD 2250. That, I realize, is still much farther in the future than you may want to hear, but remember, we are talking about **mass** acceptance of a new paradigm, not just the ideas of a "cutting edge."

One of the most important trends that is becoming increasingly evident, but is still a long way from general acceptance is the reemergence of the Goddess, with its correlating redefinition of the roles of women. In "Twelve Wings" the significance of the Goddess in the evolution of the Age of Pisces was portrayed through a class discussion:

"In our discussions of the earlier ages based on the stories of Genesis, you made much of the shift of dominance from masculine to feminine and back. Pisces should be a feminine age, but we still have a male God-figure... Let's talk about that."

"O.K., so God is still called 'he'... let's look at how clearly the gospels shifted the emphasis back to the matriarchy and the elevation of the female. God came to Moses and the Age of Aries in a burning bush and in a pillar of fire. But God came to the new age as a human baby, born of a mortal woman. Jesus loved and respected his mother, and provided for her even as he died on the cross. He pointedly set up ideals of gentleness, compassion and meekness. It was a woman, Mary Magdalene [misrepresented by some preachers to be a whore—this is NOT in the gospels] who became the first person to discover and tell the good news that Christ had risen.

"The early church reflected the shift in its elevation of Mary to the status of Queen of Heaven and Mother of God. Really, it is Mary who should be carefully reconsidered as the symbol of the proper example for humanity to follow in reaching for the ideal that was taught by Christ. The Church has made of Christ a God, forever set apart from all mortals, one with God since before the Creation... Mary would make an easier example. She was mortal, just like we are—yet she was elevated to immortality. With her we can identify. She shows that it is possible for a mere mortal to attain immortality."

"It would be even easier to identify with Mary if the church could rise above its insistence on interpreting 'Virgin' only as a literal sexual technicality and re-examine what the symbol Virgin really means."

"True! Just think of the time that has been wasted arguing over the totally unprovable assumption that Mary was a technical virgin and Jesus was conceived without the help of a mortal father. In the final analysis, why should that really matter? Would it make the lessons that Jesus taught any less valid if Joseph was someday proved to have been his natural father; or even if Jesus himself, was proven to have been married and fathered children? If one's faith in God is anchored on literal interpretations of the *Bible*, one is very vulnerable to the possibility of shattered faith when scientific evidence is offered that disproves that literal interpretation.

"But if one's faith is based on the concepts that the stories and the people of the Bible symbolize, then one's faith is much more likely to grow and evolve with each new discovery. I've no doubt that the earliest Christian writers used the symbolism of the Virgin and the Fishes, polarities of the New Age, in their narratives. Too bad the connection has been forgotten. A review of the meaning of the ancient zodiacal symbols could bring a new perspective of great value to these time in which we live."

"O.K., according to your theme of opposition, Virgo symbolizes, in this Age of Pisces, the ways in which we are bound to matter."

"And by the negative manifestation of Virgo, humanity remains separate from its vision of God; while by the virtues of Virgo, great growth in civilization and greater harmony with the collective ideal is achieved."

"What, then do we have in Mary as a symbol? Certainly she epitomizes the key phrase for Virgo, 'I serve'. In Luke, Chapter 1:26-38, we learn that the archangel Gabriel appeared to a virgin named Mary, who was betrothed to a man named Joseph of the House of David. Gabriel informed Mary that she was to bear a son who would be called 'Son of the Most High', and that God would 'give him the throne of David his father.' Mary questioned the angel as to how this could be possible, and was given the example of her kinswoman, Elizabeth, being in her sixth month of pregnancy even though she was long past child-bearing age. With that, Mary accepted the message of the angel, saying, 'I am the handmaiden of the Lord. Let it be done onto me according to thy will.'

"One can interpret these verses in a way that totally supports the early church emphasis on absolute faith and obedience to the revealed word of God. Thus we have been given, through religious art and through elaboration on the gospel story, a picture of a very young and completely innocent girl, who, with only one small, frightened question, believed the miracle of the angel's message and humbly agreed to serve as she was told. Out of this grew an image of Mary that defines Virgin (and the prime ideal for womanhood in the teachings of the church) as pure, set above the lusts of the flesh, and absolutely subservient.

"Now, I propose that this interpretation shortchanges Mary and all of womanhood with her. Let's take another look at Mary-of-the-Gospel. Are there really any words of Luke's that portray her as the least bit meek or over-awed by this person who claims to be a messenger of God? No, she speaks right up with true Virgoan discernment, saying, in essence, 'What you are telling me sounds pretty incredible. Prove it to me.' Gabriel sounds quite sure of himself, so she accepts his mission verbally while probably thinking to herself, 'That is, if what you say is true, then I'll accept it, because I do want to be of service to God.'

"Now does she go to her mother, or to her betrothed, with this fantastic story? Does she dreamily fantasize to them about her new spiritual glory? Maybe a Pisces might do that, but not our Virgin! As is stated in the very next verses of Luke, she sets out 'in haste' to visit Elizabeth. Why? It seems to me that the most likely reason is that she needed to find out if Elizabeth was truly pregnant. It was only after Elizabeth's greeting to her 'proved' the angel's story that Mary rejoiced in her own blessing with the words of the beautiful Magnificat."

"For sure," agreed a Virgo, "No true Virgo type would have swallowed the angel's story without analyzing the evidence."

"A reconsideration of the image of Mary as the primary carrier, in this age, of the archetypal Virgin of the zodiac, would give a healthier perspective on womanhood in general and on the struggle for equality of the sexes that is an issue of our times...Virgo is the zodiacal symbol of the Mother Goddess, and the most ancient personifications of deity were surely Mother. Long ago, childbirth was a major mystery. No one had figured out that men had anything to do with it. Women, who could reproduce not only their own kind, but also the opposite gender, males, were regarded with great awe. It was only natural that the first deities were goddesses. Fertility figure relics of the most ancient religions attest to the matriarchal emphasis. The main function of men was to use their superior strength for the hunt and for the protection of the women and their children. The women were the wise ones, the keepers of the mysteries, the priestesses, the nurturers of their children and of communal life. Earliest astrologies were primarily lunar, as the phases of the moon guided the seasons of planting and harvest and the hunt. And the moon was associated with woman, who gave birth anew each day to the sun. Ancient representations of goddesses often included lunar symbols—even Mary in some Christian art is portrayed standing upon the moon. The Goddess reigned supreme throughout the world as the feminine sign, Taurus, became the cardinal ascendant. During the short Age of Aries, conquering patriarchal tribes enforced the new order by the brutal slaughter of many Goddess-worshipping populations. Still, many clung tenaciously to worship of the Mother right into the transition period of the Arian to the Piscean ages. The only way that the Christians could make their new religion with its God-man palatable to conquered people, such as the Celts, was to offer Mary, Mother of God, as a substitute for their Goddess. This is largely the reason for the extreme veneration of Mary in the early church.

"Even the name, Mary, has an interesting history. I wonder if those who wrote the gospels really knew the actual name of Jesus' mother, or if the name was chosen for its symbolic meaning?"

"What do you mean?"

"Mary comes from the root 'mar', which in Indo-European languages is 'the sea'. The pre-Christian goddess, Mari, was Goddess of the Sea, the Great Fish who gave birth to the gods, sometimes pictured in the form of a mermaid. The Latin form of Mary, Maria, means 'the seas'. Even the name of Mary's mother, Anna, is a form of the pre-Christian 'grandmother goddess'. She was the crone of the female trinity: virgin, mother, crone. As Di-Ana (divine Ana), she was mother of Mari. In other language variations this creatress-goddess was called Anu, Nana or Inanna."[13]

"I just had an interesting thought! Christian doctrine may preach a man-god, but Christian intuition must be more comfortable with the Mother. Think of all the notable visions and miracles of Mary—like at Fatima and at Lourdes. I can't think of any comparable visions of Jesus. When supernatural visions of deity appear in this age, they are female!"

"You're right! I hadn't thought about it that way before. Fascinating..."

"Why, then, in this age of the Pisces-Virgo feminine polarity have women been so severely suppressed by the church? Why has the full potential of womanhood remained so repressed and distorted in our culture?"

"One reason is probably that our action principle in this age, our cardinal ascendant, is Aries. Our ideal, the Word that must be spread (mutable) is Piscean; but action is initiated (cardinal) with the expression of Aries. Jesus, a key teacher for this age, understood and exemplified the highest expression of Aries, and Pisces, and of all the other signs for that matter. But the end of the Arian Age found most of humanity entrenched in a world view that expressed Aries at its macho-masculine worst. The struggle for patriarchal dominance was won and God was unequivocally male. Only man was created in his image. Jesus tried to soften people's concept of God into an always forgiving father figure, but the new religion was rooted in the fiery, masculine, punishing God-concept of the Arian Age. World views change very slowly. A new concept (like the teachings of Jesus) may be accepted in theory, but those who must act to spread the new concept have unconscious motivations carried over from the old ways. (Witness the un-Christ-like wars, slaughters and heretic burnings of the early churchmen's actions that they claimed were done in the name of spreading the teachings of Christ.) Women were little more than pieces of property by the end of the Arian Age, so despite the prominence of the Marys in the gospel, women were given only the most subservient of roles in the organization of the new religion.

"Probably the main zodiacal explanation, though, for the suppression and distortion of feminine potential is because it is the

---

[13] More information about Goddess religions can be found in *God Herself*, Geraldine Thorston, Avon Books, 1980; *When God Was A Woman*, Merlin Stone, Harves/HBJ, 1976; *The Women's Encyclopedia of Myths and Secrets*, Barbara Walker, Harper & Row, 1983.

Virgin, herself, who is now the symbol of opposition to our Piscean vision of deity. Once upon a time a Goddess, she is now only a mortal and fit to be saved only by the benevolence of a Father God. However virtuous the maiden might be, she is still the descendant of Eve, who according to the authors of Aries-time, led man to his downfall...

For centuries, the collective society of mortals acted out its distorted and suppressed and misunderstood Virgo. Her earthy sensuality was considered an evil rather than a virtue. Her ability to think with creativity and wisdom was devalued in favor of the emphasis on unquestioning faith. Her capacity for discernment was distorted into a nit-picking, fussy-with-details intolerance that caused the splintering of the religion her son founded into hundreds of quarreling sects. It was as if she was bound in slavery, rather than in service. When the symbolic pendulum swung from the pole of Revelation/Faith to the pole of Reason in the 18th century, the suppressed slave began her escape.

"One who is suppressed for all that time is likely to emerge a very angry lady! Her intellect so rebelled against the old requirement of obedient faith, that spiritual values were denied in favor of total dominance by materialistic science. Society still suffers from the effects of her rebellion, though in this latter 20th century, some signs of movement toward balance are beginning to be seen, particularly in the new consideration by scientific leaders of matters of the spirit and the intangible. Also very hopeful are recent ecumenical movements among Christian denominations; and tolerance—-even interest—in blending some of the ideas of eastern religions with those of the west.

"The problems caused by the severe repression of sexuality, and of women in general, are still very much with us. Suppressed sexuality erupted into an over-blown, over-emphasized pornographic version of sex that denies its spiritual nature and purpose.

... Much will be gained in the spiritualization of Virgo that is necessary to reach for the ideals of Pisces, when we collectively realize that society must place the highest priority values on the functions that are of the nature of the Mother Goddess. No material concern, no mark of status, should ever be placed before the nurturing and education of our young, and the feeding of our hungry!"

"You're really on a soapbox, aren't you?"

"Yes, I suppose so. But one of my pet peeves is the low status accorded to the full-time mother and the elementary school teacher, when the work they do is more important than anything else to the future of society. Mark my words, great changes will take place before this age comes to a close. Pisces/Virgo is a feminine polarity. The Holy Mother will yet see her daughters returned not only to

equality, but to positions of great respect. And take heed, fathers of
the church [Catholic]... You've denied her daughters the right to
serve as her 'high priestesses'. This will change and must change.
Your ability to recognize this, and welcome female priests, may well
be a major deciding factor on whether the church as we know it will
fall, or move forward into Age of Aquarius...

With the perspective of 15 years since I wrote "Twelve
Wings," I'd add emphasis on the concept of Earth as Mother,
and the increasing awareness that the old patriarchal "rape" of
the Earth Mother must give way to respect for and protection
of her. This, too, is a reflection of the evolution of the concerns
of the feminine in this Piscean Age.

The dominance of male deities in this age is not a reflection
of Pisces symbolism, but rather of the fact that the age began
in a time of extreme male dominance, an outgrowth of the
Arian age paradigm. This is gradually changing, just as Pisces
is gradually becoming the cardinal ascendant. Will astrology
change, too, to reflect this? I think it will. Little glimmers of
change already appear, just as the mass concepts of "right"
action in our society are beginning to very gradually shift from
masculine to feminine values. It's slow, to be sure, but I am
amused by the number of times, in the past few years, I've
noticed art portraying the Aquarian Waterbearer as a woman,
rather than the traditional man. How appropriate, to think of
Pisces Rising, ascendancy of the Goddess, as herald for the
Aquarian Age!

The Future of the Age of Pisces...

What are our collective ideals? Our true spiritual leaders of all
faiths, everywhere, speak of love of neighbor, compassion, selfless-
ness, sacrifice—Piscean virtues all.

Virgo symbolizes our reality and Virgo is notorious for "missing
the forest for the trees." Are we so caught up in mountains of trivia,
in narrow fields of specialty, in details of living in our own small
space on the planet, that we have lost sight of the wholeness of our
vision?

An astrology text might describe the faults of Pisces as lack of
firm principles, vacillation, self-delusion, escapism, and a superficial sentimentality in place of true empathy. Do these not sound like
familiar ills of society in these times?

Our most technologically advanced civilizations express materialistic Virgo at the height of efficiency. But in the process, our very humanity is reduced to a computer number. A vast proportion of our technology is used to build weaponry that threatens to reduce our humanity to ashes. Small wonder that escapism is rampant.

In this time period, as never before, it is important to pause and reflect upon why we are building these things—or permitting them to be built by our silent acquiescence to those who hold positions of power. Our technology should serve the spirit and vision of humanity, not threaten to destroy it.

In the reality of our physical world, we humans come in many varied kinds—and how our Virgoan minds love to categorize and discriminate and criticize others' differences. We differ in color, in nationality, in religion, in education, in language, in size, in taste—the list could go on and on. But suppose we actually visited by a race of extra-terrestrials? Would we seem as different from each other to them—or would they simply regard us as all members of one species? Should we not concentrate our energy into discovering the ways in which we are similar? Perhaps, then, empathy and compassion would come more easily, and fears would diminish...

Within this time will we have the war to end all wars, or will we decide to end the potential for a war of total world destruction by disarming? Either alternative would mean a re-birth—a new beginning. Let us project that the decision to disarm can be reached through initiative, rather than through response to the devastation of a third world war.

We live in a time in which change and upheaval on a massive scale is truly to be expected. Our technology has made this so. Events in any part of the world can be instantly transmitted throughout the world, touching the lives of billions. Most of these events pass in and out of our consciousness, having only a passing effect. But we are vulnerable now, and far more linked to everyone else than ever before in history. The economic collapse of one country, even a small one, would domino its effects all over the world. A nuclear attack—or accident—anywhere could start a chain reaction that could threaten everyone. The health of present and future generations of millions could be threatened by a mistake, an accident, or an irresponsible use of chemicals. There is no question that our attitudes of separateness, of opposition, of "us vs. them" must change. The only question is how much punishment we will bring upon our world before we realize that we are all in it together.

Progress already! At the time I wrote that, "the bomb" was still the major millennial threat—the cold war very much a "hot" issue. The fact that it no longer is gives me even more hope for this world of ours. Twenty-some years ago I remember grave astrological and psychic predictions that Pluto's transit through Scorpio would bring about a nuclear holocaust. Instead, it was during that transit that the cold war ended and disarmament began. Perhaps all those prayers for peace that were synchronized around the world had something to do with it. We change our consciousness and we can change our world. Believe it! Don't be a negative Piscean victim, fearing the millennium and "heading for the hills." Be a Piscean mystic and a dreamer who develops the practical Virgoan skills to make your dreams manifest! The ills of society will change when enough people stop blaming and start looking around for what they can personally do to make things better. I repeat my "Twelve Wings" prediction that:

> ... about 2025 AD... will be a time in which great masses of people can rise out of the mire of separatism and opposition that has characterized this epoch...I see...2025-2475 as a kind of New Renaissance, but more glorious than the last. Science will continue to advance, but now with a new sense of humanitarian purpose for its progress. New emphasis will be given to all of the humanities—to all fields of study that nourish the spirit of humanity. The arts will flourish as never before. Chastised by the past upheavals that were caused by greed and separatism, those of us who still remain, and those who were born and brought up during the upheaval, will have new values, and renewed vision. The practical realities of Virgo will again be given balance by the mystical vision of Pisces. The pendulum is at the fulcrum—but soon to swing out again.

The Age of Aquarius

Our imaginary pendulum has again reached an outermost point of its swing—but now that point is Scorpio, [square to] the top of the cross [symbol of the new vision], Aquarius. It is the Age of Aquarius.

...The end of the old order overlaps the beginning of the new. [By the time the constellation of Aquarius rises with the Sun at vernal equinox] the vision of the new order will be firmly established. And the seeds of conflict with its opposing forces will be planted. For now, those who have mastered the lessons of Pisces will have already accepted the highest ideals of Aquarius, and will be at peace with their universe. For those still struggling [with Piscean fears and us vs. them dualism] ... all is chaos. If peace with one's fellows cannot be found on this small planet, how will one ever deal with Aquarius?

Aquarius symbolizes the breaking of boundaries. The Waterbearer pours out the waters and sets the fishes free. The fish that swims in the waters of the constellation Aquarius is not bound by a cord as were the fishes of Pisces. It is free—physically free to leave the circle of the ecliptic and explore the entire cosmos! In the Age of Aquarius, travel in outer space will no longer be just the experiments of a few. It will be the experience of many. The cycle of time for our earth and its passengers will still be marked by our cosmic clock of the zodiac—but now many humans will break free of that clock and move on to places where other zodiacs and other concepts of time will prevail. How naive to think that the faces of God (the whole) are twelve. God has infinite expressions—yet all belong to the Whole... Still "fish", still swimming in the waters of earthly mortality, the children of Aquarius will find that the outer limitations of that mortality are far more distant than their ancestors ever imagined. Boundaries will be broken for those who remain in residence on Earth, too, as the potentials of the human brain are explored and expanded.

New archeological finds will unlock ancient mysteries. Visitors from other worlds will bring new concepts. The capacity of the human brain will be found to encompass phenomena now thought to be supernatural. Astral projection, levitation, telepathic communication will be so commonplace that they will be routinely taught to school children.

All of these new developments will assist the spiritual teachers of Aquarius to prove that all gods are One. Not just one Messiah will come to the Age of Aquarius, but many... In equal proportion the teachers will be men and women of every race and of every ethnic background. They will bring the same message. They will point out the same Truth that underlies faiths of ages past. In unity with each other they will cause all religious boundaries to melt away—and all ethnic and nationalistic boundaries as well. All, in the center of Being, are One.

With Pisces rising, as the cardinal ascendant, Mary as Mother Goddess, could well be the most popular personification of deity, but no violent struggles will enforce that choice. In the new enlightenment of the masses in this age, it will be understood both intuitively (Pisces) and intellectually (Aquarius) that all gods are One. Christ will be revered by all, but not in a manner forever set apart from human potential, but as a personification of the fulfillment of every soul's destiny to return to unity with God. A new name will be chosen to express the universality of the new world religion.

The new religion will so influence the mass consciousness that discrimination based on one's heredity and cultural environment can finally vanish. No longer will sex or color or background be a factor of acceptable limitation to one's achievements. Only excellence of the mind (an ideal of the new "airy" paradigm) will count.

The scene just painted may sound like Utopia to many readers, but a nightmare to others. In either case, it is only a part of the potential expression of Aquarius...

Aquarius, no more than any other constellation, makes a wonderful ideal if we speak only of his virtues—of freedom, of humanitarianism, of universal truth. Aquarius is an air sign, associated with the intellect or Mind. Yet he bears water, associated with the Spirit. So, we could imagine a blending of Mind with Spirit, as the highest human intellect, having discovered Universal Truth, pours out the waters of Spirit to nourish all.

Certainly, these ideals will be presented to humanity by the great teachers who will emerge during the centuries of transition.

But Aquarian ideals, no less than those of other constellations, can be corrupted. The faults of Aquarius, and the characteristics of Leo, its opposition; as well as the extremes that might be characteristic of its "insurgent" squares, Scorpio and Taurus, can provide clues to the ways in which the Age of Aquarius will fall short of Utopia.

As the Age of Aquarius begins, the wheel will have shifted and our imaginary pendulum will strike the Scorpio arm of the new cross that humanity must bear.

Scorpio is the sign of death and regeneration. Among its characteristics are a capacity for deep, probing research and a tendency to be manipulative and a need to control. Scorpio will sacrifice personal possessions to take care of others—often whether the others want that kind of help or not.

Aquarius is a revolutionary that breaks boundaries of the mind and idealizes Universal Truth. But Aquarius Truth is for all—for the humanitarian needs of the group. Aquarius can be quite detached from the feelings of the individual. So what is right for the group? And who will decide?

The birth pangs of the Age of Aquarius will include the new reality that in order to achieve the vision of Equality of rights and liberty for all, somebody has to organize the masses. The new reality is symbolized by Leo the Lion of Dominion. A government will emerge that will organize all of the people of the world into one democratic unit. The new government will not come to power through nuclear war as that threat will have been resolved centuries before. This government will be given power by acclamation of the people because its leaders have demonstrated an ability to improve the lives of the people. Such extensive freedoms will have been achieved in the New Renaissance and transitory centuries that anarchy will prevail all over the world. Not enough people will grasp the Piscean vision of Love Thy Neighbor.

Too many people will accept the new religion on a superficial level only. Bound by material values, society will discover that too much freedom means that no one is free. Weary of the struggle to survive against others whose idea of freedom infringes upon one's own, the people will be ripe for Scorpion manipulation and control. An Aquarian oligarchy will be ready for them and ready to use all the powers of Scorpio; just as over two millenniums before, the Piscean church leaders had used the dogmatism of Sagittarius to establish their vision with the masses.

Scorpio issues of death and birth and genetics will be researched extensively and manipulated toward the goal of equality that represents the ideal of the oligarchy and of the people who elect it and give it power. Individual creativity (Leo) and the right to individual possessions (Taurus) will be suppressed, perhaps severely, for the sake of the needs of the whole group. No one must be hungry, everyone must have a job, a place to live. How can this be accomplished? Brave New World? Huxley's vision will be scientifically possible by this time.[14]

[Huxley's vision of a world dominated by genetic engineering also had most people spending much of their time zoned out on a drug called Soma as a form of escape. This could be a manifestation of the overlay of Pisces as the cardinal, action principle in the Age of Aquarius.)

But the cosmic clock will move on. Individual freedom cannot be suppressed forever... The oligarchy will be stopped before the nightmare of Brave New World can be achieved; and the problems of burgeoning population will be solved by the colonization of other worlds. Taurus can again acquire and take root and build. And Leo will be encouraged to create with joy and bring up an abundance of children to populate the universe...

Resolution? Happy ever after? No, I went on with an astrological sci-fi flavored look at ages yet to come. Space doesn't permit them all, but here's a peek at the Age of Capricorn (c. AD 4500) according to the movement of vernal point through the constellations), at which point, in spite of enlightened science in the Age of Aquarius, I projected Mother Earth finally losing her patience:

... She announces her exasperation with her children by bringing in the Age of Capricorn with catastrophic earthquakes and Arian (Aries, the "insurgent" square) volcanic eruptions at "Mount Sinais" all over the world. Weather conditions wreak havoc everywhere. Land ruined by accumulated chemical manipulation will no

---

[14] Aldous Huxley, *Brave New World*, New York: Harper Brothers, 1932.

longer bear healthy crops, and the contamination of the land affects animal life, too. Some species of insects, birds, and animals that were once thought harmless, mutate out of control and become dangerous. Insect infestations cause people to again think of the ancient Biblical prophecies and wonder if the tribulation is finally at hand. Even the ever-purifying oceans have become dangerously polluted. The people are forced to much greater use of chemical substitutes for the ruined natural food supply; but the extensive unnatural manipulation of nutrition results in new diseases for both humans and animals.

The world government oligarchy will acknowledge, too late, that massive changes must take place. Earth may have to be abandoned completely, they speculate. But that is impossible—there are still billions here. The cost! It can't be done! The people clamor for protection; the leaders bicker among themselves about what to do, who is to blame, whose ideas should prevail. The oligarchy will collapse and a dictator will take control, and raise a powerful police force to try to bring order out of chaos.

But for the first time in many centuries, the instant communication all over the world that made central government possible will be broken down by Mother Earth's rebellion. Natural disasters will cut off groups of people from the rest of the world, and all happens too much, too fast for the central government to handle. In the absence of tight central control, rival leaders will take charge in various areas and challenge the central dictator. As people gather into groups for protection, separate nations will gradually begin to emerge.

Some people, previously reluctant to immigrate to other worlds, will now try to leave and escape the chaos on earth, and some will succeed. But with the breakdown of central control, and the extensive cost of dealing with the problems of earth, space travel will decrease. And earth's colonies on other worlds will lessen their contacts with their former home, choosing to avoid risk at the hands of rival dictators and their police forces.

Some groups will gather under truly responsible leaders who will be able to organize the people into efforts that will restore the natural resources of their area. This will be a true "back-to-nature" movement, as people research and rediscover how to live off the land. Life will be difficult for people accustomed to the push-button, automated world of Aquarius, but in many areas, there will be no choice....

Astrologers, who in the Aquarian Age were mainly concerned with heliocentric and galactic-centered concepts, and detailed mathematical abstractions; will now return to earth-centered basics. Deprived of their computers in many weather ravaged areas, they will relearn how to look at the sky; and they will research ancient writings on dusty shelves of neglected libraries, and try to piece together their heritage from a human and a religious perspective.

The cosmic clock will turn onward, in this time of the cross of Capricorn. Eventually, the Arian square that brought a return to aggressive conflict will find its Libran balance and become the pioneering spirit that helps meet the challenge to protect the home (Cancer) with the ideal of Capricorn responsibility. The goat can climb the mountain.

Over two thousand years from now for the massive earth changes that could throw civilization back to a primitive state? When people have been warning me for over 20 years to get out of California because it was going to fall into the ocean? Well I make no claims of infallibility. I could be wrong, and I do most certainly support ecological measures to preserve and honor Mother Earth. Let's just say that in recapping these "Twelve Wings" projections, according to the symbolism of the Great Ages, I hope to add to the general tone of this book that predictions of catastrophe in the early 21st century need to be placed within a broader perspective.

Look around at the proliferation of dire predictions for the Millennium. Fear sells! Why is it that so many people seem to want to believe the worst? I could characterize it as one more unproductive expression of Piscean confusion. Pisces is also the sign of the mystic. Instead of giving in to fear, let's take a mystical, magical approach and visualize the coming of that New Renaissance, and do the best we can to move our world in that direction.

There is no reason to fear the onset of the 21st century. Question the motives of those who try to tell you differently. Fear not only sells, but it serves the purposes of those who seek to control—to maintain or achieve power over others. Will disasters happen at the turn of the millennium? Probably. What year does **not** include some kind of disaster somewhere? If you're in the middle of it, it seems like the end of the world, at least for a while. If you're across the country from it, it's a passing news story. Some people will dwell on their role as victims, but many others will pitch in to help others and rebuild, restoring the faith of everyone around them in the best of human nature. So much of anything in life is a matter of perspective. I know of no real good that has ever come of predicting—and focusing on—potential catastrophe. Instead do whatever you can to develop the knowledge, the skills and the inner strength to direct your own destiny, and to respond effectively to the events you didn't plan.

God/Goddess dwells within you! Claim that power within to move ahead with your dreams and create a better future for yourself and others!

Predictions for the Ages—Long Range

First, to recap my long-range predictions based on the Ages of the Zodiac, which were contained within the text of the previous article (because I know many readers will just scan for the predictions—there's more detail and background in the text):

- A "golden age," which I've called the New Renaissance, begins around AD 2025, comes into full flower at about AD 2250, and continues until about AD 2475. During these centuries all fields of learning that nourish the spirit of humanity will be greatly emphasized. An enlightened science will flourish in harmony and balance with the arts and spirituality, recognizing the necessity of both faith and reason to a healthy, wholistic society. For the most part, a materialistic society will have regained a spiritual center.

- A deeper realization of our world-wide independence will begin to banish separatism, and new values and visions will emerge within the masses, leading toward greater tolerance and cooperation.

- Feminine issues involving the nurturing and educating of children, and the nurturing of the Earth will come into greater prominence. Women in positions of leadership will be common, rather than unusual. The concept of a Mother/Father God or Goddess as a proper personification of deity will be widely accepted. Mary, in a new and richer interpretation as Mother Goddess will be even more popular with the masses.

- The true dawning of the Age of Aquarius (around AD 2600) comes with a period of anarchy (Aquarian rebellion), coupled with a move (Scorpio square) within the scientific and economic realms to use genetic research for manipulation and control. The masses could be kept appeased with widespread use of drugs (shades of Huxley's *Brave New World*).

- As society begins to crumble worldwide, the nations, realizing that too much freedom means no one is free, will elect an oligarchy to organize a one-world government. The oligarchy (in the symbolism of Aquarius) will place the needs of the whole in such priority that individual creativity (Leo), including the procreation of children, is suppressed, along with the right to individual possessions (Taurus).

- As humanity moves fully into the Age of Aquarius (AD 2700-2800), human travel to colonize distant planets becomes a reality—breaking the boundaries of Earth (and its zodiac). For those who remain on Earth, boundaries of the mind will be broken, as phenomena now thought to be supernatural, such as astral projection, levitation, and telepathic communication will be so commonplace as to be taught to school children.

- A new world religion will grow out of the teachings of multiple male and female "messiahs" from every race and ethnic background, who will point out that the same Truth underlies faiths of the past, and all in the center of being, are One. As a result, discrimination based on sex, color or background will vanish. The only distinguishing matter that will still set people apart will be excellence of the mind (an ideal of the "airy" Aquarian paradigm).

- Individual freedom will not be suppressed for long. The initially suppressive oligarchy will be replaced with a more democratic government. The problems of burgeoning population will be, in part, solved by the colonization of other worlds.

- It is with the onset of the earthy paradigm of the Age of Capricorn (c. AD 4500) that I projected a time of truly catastrophic worldwide rebellion from Mother Earth, with massive earthquakes, volcanic eruptions, and horrible weather conditions everywhere, responding to an environment ruined through the accumulated effects of greed and chemical manipulation. Too far ahead to think about? I don't think so. This is a scenario that could as easily be the final shot of Virgoan Earth Mother in this age, if we don't begin now to take seriously our responsibility to protect her, and if we can't come to terms with the core concepts of love that are the Piscean vision.

Predictions from 1998 through the Turn of the Century

In deference to the promise of this book to predict (with the implication of the year 2000 and the few years after that, rather than hundreds of years from now), I'll close with some additional thoughts about potential events based on current mundane charts.[15] I predict that:

- President Clinton's chart, generally, is in a good cycle, so he will most likely prevail politically in spite of opponents' attempts to bring him down. Still, he'll have major hassles in regard to a prominent female (or females) in 1998 (which is hardly surprising—there are multiple candidates). The issues involving females are particularly in focus around the time of the Solar Eclipse conjunct his Sun in August.

     During his last year in office, he'll strongly feel the sense of being a "lame duck."

- The situation in Baghdad is increasingly unstable in '98. Hussein feels alone in the world and very frustrated. He could face rebellion or assassination.

- More 1998 financial failures in Japan will lead to the suicide of prominent leader(s), and ultimately to a change in their government.

- The coming of the year 2000 will be primarily marked by lots of media hype. No matter that it isn't really the beginning of the 21st century! (Since the 2000 year count began with one, the year 2000 is really the last year of the 20th century). There's just something, somehow, magical about all those numbers turning over at once, just like watching the odometer on your car! The media and people's wish for,

---

[15] For those readers who are concerned about techniques; I am basing my predictions on several charts that are customary to the study of mundane astrology: Winter Solstice for 1999 and 2000 (entry of the Sun into 0° Capricorn marks the annual rebirth of the Sun), Spring Equinox for 1999 and 2000 (entry of the Sun into 0° Aries marks the Sun's return to the beginning of the zodiac), Solar Eclipse charts previous to the beginning of the years 2000 and 2001, and the charts for midnight January 1, 2000 and January 1, 2001. I am primarily looking at the cardinal axis on the 90° dial, a technique of Uranian astrology, or in the case of the eclipse charts, the eclipse point (Sun/Moon conjunction). In some cases, I have also considered the Midheaven and Ascendant positions for Washington, D.C.

of fear of, that magic will make the year 2000 the turn of the millennium, even if it is not.

- The approach of January 1, 2000, will be accompanied by a monument amount of tension as:

- A few religious/spiritual extremist groups will isolate themselves, waiting for the end

- Religious ideology will become increasingly polarized, with more extremists willing to take actions that are decidedly against their own core religious doctrines in order to impose their will on "unbelievers."

- Scam artists will be out in force, seeking to capitalize by preying on millennial fears

- Most people will express their hopes, and suppress their fears or nagging doubts, as they plan various special New Year's celebrations:

- A fair number of people will take the hedonistic route and party to the extravagant extreme, feeling that if it's the end, they might as well go out with a bang

- Great influxes of tourists, seeking the "higher road" (just in case) will flock to various major religious sites or new age power places, there to await the countdown.

- Charts for after the turn of the century look more upbeat than those preceding it. When January 1, 2000, has come and gone, most of us will still be here, neither Jesus nor the aliens having appeared. Most people will turn their thoughts to getting on with their lives, and creating new things, excited about being among those present in the new millennium.

- Still, some will be disappointed, and assisted by a media that had previously shunned technical types' reminders that the century really doesn't start until 2001, they'll grasp at the idea that "it's really next year" and start the millennial countdown all over again.

- A strong female leader will emerge in US politics during 1999. The year 2000 could see her as a presidential contender. Although many will support her, others will be extremely upset. A fanatic group could target her for assassination—an attempt that won't succeed. Though the situation does not look particularly good for her in the spring of 2000, the November election could give the USA its first female president.

- The strong female influence (that triggered my above thought) is significant to the world in general, not just the USA. Though a first female president would certainly fit that criterion, there are two other potentials (that seem currently unlikely, but hey, I can hope!). These are: sainthood for Mother Theresa, and the elevation by the Roman Catholic Church of Mary to Co-Redeemer.

- The turn of the century will see the death of an important political alliance, and the emergence of a significant new alliance. This will create changes that affect the entire world

- A major concern of the masses will be a new and widespread illness, infection or virus. It is possible that this could be in connection with a chemical warfare bacteria. The United States, as we move toward the latter part of the year 2000, will take the lead in fighting and overcoming this threat, and in the process, increase its worldwide standing as protector. The female leader will be a central figure in this.

- At, or very close to, the turn of the century the throne of England will pass to Prince Charles, and there will be a new Pope in Rome.

Astrology Looks At The New Millennium

Astrology And The Concept of Seasons

One of my favorite ways to teach an introductory class is to begin by describing astrology as simply a system that's akin to the quite-accepted science of meteorology—on a much grander scale. Meteorologists, after all, spend their time studying seasonal patterns, finding the repetition in those patterns—as well as the anomalies—and making predictions based on their studies. As astrologers, we're much like our meteorological cousins (although not too many of them would admit it, I'll bet). Basically, we use what we already know from cycles of the past to judge what to expect from the future. This same technique is how El Nino's potent effects were predicted by Them—and how Ann E. Parker makes her amazingly accurate earthquake predictions for Us. The major difference between Us and Them is that astrologers recognize the value of the seasons of all of the planets— while meteorologists restrict themselves to the cycles of the Sun, and, occasionally, the Moon.

Natal Astrology Vs. Mundane Astrology

Of course, there are other factors that separate us. For example, astrologers use research on the planetary 'seasons' to judge individual personality traits. We erect charts that freeze-frame the heavenly bodies at the moment of a person's birth, add the perspective of time and location by setting the Earth at the center, and are able to see where each planet (and every heavenly body, in fact) was from the individual's point of view. Thus, we create a map of the Universe with the individual at the center, a 'circular lens' of sorts through which the individual views the world like no one else—the horoscope. Although we necessarily take into account that people have their own unique agendas, along with the free will to use their planetary 'tools' as they see fit, it's still quite possible to do some legitimate 'predictions' of personality traits and upcoming events in someone's life, based on these charts. You can't do that with meteorology.

Astrologers also have options meteorologists don't. We have the ability to make an extremely educated guess as to what the future holds, on a larger scale, by observing the cycles of the Outer Planets, Uranus, Neptune, and Pluto. Although the patterns of all the planets are useful, both on an individual level and as a gauge to decide which types of trends to expect on a global level, the Outers are especially helpful to create a wide-angle view for humanity, since their locations so far out in the solar system make their orbits much longer than the Inner Planets. Uranus, for example, takes 84 years to complete an orbit, Neptune takes 165 years, and Pluto circles the Sun in 248 years. Pluto, then, can hover in one degree for up to four months, while Mars averages about ³/₄ of a degree per day, and our Moon covers a degree in roughly 2 ½ hours. The Outer Planets, then, are the ones mundane astrologers watch. More on that later.

Isn't Mundane Astrology 'Boring'?

Now, speaking of Mundane Astrology, let's get something straight. The word 'mundane' has a bad reputation, traditionally conjuring up images of wizened old men in leather straight-back chairs, hiding behind the financial section of *The Times*. It's also a word that's associated with something that's so 'normal' as to be boring. In truth, however, Mundane Astrology is far from boring. It's the branch of astrology that examines long-term planetary trends—the 'fads' and collective attitudes that make one generation unique from the next. Mundane also looks at the charts of countries, and the leaders who sit behind the steering wheel of these major entities. It's also the branch of our craft that's concerned with the planetary combinations that inspire the major events which impact life for all of us here on Planet Number Three on a collective level—the instant Neil Armstrong first set foot on the Moon, the moment the first blow was struck to the Berlin Wall, or the time that a declaration of War was issued. Needless to say, then, the debut of a brand-new century is one of those monumental moments that's far from boring, and fascinating to Mundane Astrologers—and a chart done up for the time it arrives will tell us a great deal about what to expect from the next 1000 years.

The New Millennium—What Does It Really Mean?

Well, first of all, remember that this isn't just a new century— it's the start of ten of them. A New Millennium. To really understand what can happen over the course of ten centuries, think of what we've seen happen over the last three alone. The 1900s brought the arrival of the automobile, two World Wars, and the ability for humans to actually step foot on the Moon. The 1800s birthed the first telegraph message, the use of anesthesia, and the end of slavery. Our country, now the undeniable world-leader in most categories, was born in the 1700s, as were the first bifocal spectacles and the first daily newspaper. All of those things were amazing—in their time— and all of those things are quite humdrum to those of us living now. Needless to say, the upcoming years will play host to discoveries and events those of us living through them will see as equally astounding. Again, however, this is the start of a whole new thousand-year period. And there's something about changing that first digit that's also going to change our mass attitude. It's inevitable. We're all waiting with bated breath to see what discoveries and events will come along with this new digit—and we've all got extremely high expectations. Colonization of Mars, cloning, and virtual reality are among the wonders we've already seen peeking over 2000s horizon, but there's much more. We've learned, over the past 1000 years, that anything is possible—that we can do it, make it, or experience it, if we can dream it. As a result, science and technology will be trying to 'live up to' the huge expectations the citizens of the world have put upon them. And they'll very likely succeed.

Inner and Outer Planets

One of the first ways to gauge what an upcoming time period will bring, especially one of so many years, is to start by looking at the positions of all the planets at the moment that new time period arrives—both by sign and through the angular relationships they'll create with each other. Now, I like to think of each of the planets as being Department Heads, and of the Sun as the Executive Director of the corporation, since he's at the center of the universe, the Big Boss all the planets revolve around. Both the Inner Planets and the Outer Planets are the heads of some very important departments, and all have a job to do. In a long-term sense, however, it's best to start by looking at the Outer Planets, The Change Makers. I call them this because, of all the planets, it's the Outers who symbolically inspire The Big Stuff. They all have a 'Make Things Change' clause built into their planetary contracts, and although their techniques are quite different, their end results are the same. On an individual level, they represent our ability to make sweeping changes, to birth ourselves over and again throughout our lives, not really seeing the new forms we've created until the process they represent is finished. Collectively, they endow us with the ability to evolve. And what's 'evolution' really all about? Adapting. It's about shedding old skin—molting, really—and replacing it with new attitudes, (and new body-shapes, if you think about what early man looked like) that allow our species to go on living in an environment that's also gradually changing. Needless to say, then, if you're looking at a long period of time, the Outers are the place to start.

All that said, let's first talk about the official titles of each of the Outer Planets, and the job responsibilities that accompany their titles.

Uranus—The Mad Professor

Uranus is the planet that's connected with futuristic thinking. He's a genius who makes his discoveries by not being afraid to break the rules, or consider a different way to do something— no matter what the traditional method has been. He's the Head of the Department of Science, Technology, Revolutions, and Rebellions—all of which are very necessary to our advancement as a species. He's also quite fond of Space—and he doesn't see it as The Final Frontier, either, only one of many frontiers he'll inspire us to explore by tugging at our curiosity and daring us to come up with tools and machines that outdo what's already in use. His orbit is 84 years—or one nice, long human life.

Neptune—The Goddess of Sighs

Neptune is a lovely goddess in a pink gown who smoothes the rough edges off of reality by choosing to see it differently. She fills in the blanks of What We Don't Know by creating her own version of the story—and it's often a romanticized version. She believes in a kinder, gentler world, and since The Real World (what Saturn affectionately refers to as 'reality') isn't always kind and gentle, she's not above creating her own version of reality—and escaping into it via fantasy, drugs, or trance. As dreamy as she is, she's the perfect lady to put in charge of passing out such heady drugs as Confusion, Idealism, and Spirituality. In fact, she's Head of the Department of these and all 'Altered States', and the earthly things that inspire them— Drugs, Alcohol, Glamour, The Arts, Fashion, and Religion, to name a few. It's her job to dissolve the boundaries of the reality that's been built around us, to gently ease us away from it by erasing it, a little at a time. She's also quite good at inspiring a generation to romanticize, idealize, and downright worship the qualities of the sign she's currently occupying. She makes her way around the Sun in about 165 years—or two loops in Uranus-time.

Pluto—The Dark Dude

Of all the Outer Planets, Pluto is the one with the least enviable job description. He's Head of the Department of Death, Decay, Destruction, and Sexual Attitudes—none of which make for light, cheery dinner conversation, all of which are quite necessary to keep life fresh and new. He's a dark figure in an even darker cloak, bringing us pretty heavy thoughts, when he visits individually. His blunt, stark way of bringing us face to face with The Inevitable conjures up images of our own mortality and the futility of our existence, on the one hand. But he also provides us with the knowledge that change—and accepting it—is one of those inevitables, and he inspires us symbolically to kick those major changes into gear. He's the ancient God of the Underworld, but in truth, he's simply the driver of the vehicle that brings along Process—especially the process of birth, death, and rebirth. He's responsible for a generation's collective attitudes about death, (and therefore abortion, physician-assisted suicide, etc.), sexuality, and Recycling—a physical representation of the Process of life, death, and rebirth. He orbits the Sun in about 248 years—about 3 cycles of Uranus.

Now, you can see that all the Outers have very important jobs to do, both individually and collectively. Ordinarily, they're invaluable for predicting long-term—but, then, what's 'long' in the eyes of humans isn't 'long' at all in the eyes of the Solar System. Think of it this way: over the next 1000 years, even far-away Pluto will have a chance to make four complete loops around the Sun. He was last in his current position around 1750, and you can see that an awful lot has happened since then—on many levels. Without the benefit of knowing the advancements that just the first of his cycles will bring, it's impossible to conceive of what the fourth will be like. Could anyone back in 1500—or 1250—or 1000—have predicted the Revolutionary War? (Besides Nostradamus, I mean). So although it's possible to predict what his costume-changes over the next century will inspire, we can only work with what we already know—and the total change he symbolically inspires is far too sweeping to discuss it in the context of 1000 years—four cycles. Since Neptune will circle the Sun about 6 times in the next 1000 years, and Uranus will make about 12 loops, trying to look at every orbit of all three won't be much help, either, not in terms of trying to predict what each cycle will bring, at least.

The Chart For The New Millennium

No, when you're looking at a period of time this sweeping, you've got to do it by looking at the birth-chart of the entity, where experience has taught us the total picture lies. After all, on an individual level, it's a fact that nothing can ever happen to us if it's not described in our birth-charts. Each horoscope is a tool-kit of sorts, reflecting what tasks the owner is equipped to handle—on the job. Lottery-winners have charts that describe sudden windfalls. Plane-crash victims have charts that describe 'sudden trips' (and that's what death is, after all—the ultimate 'long-trip'), and politicians have charts that speak of purveying mass-power. In a nutshell, whatever occurs in our lifetimes has got to have an Honorable Mention in our birth-charts—or it won't come to pass. And the same 'rule' holds true for the Big Picture. It's why Mundane Astrologers look so carefully at ingresses and lunations—to see what to expect from the entity created by a period of time.

All that said, let's take a look at the chart for January, 1, 2000, at 12:00 AM. The start of a new year, a new century, and a New Millennium. We'll set the chart's location for Washington, D.C., since, (at this writing, at least), our nation's capital is where most of the changes that will affect us will begin. We'll start with Pluto, and work our way in, narrowing our focus as we go, using what we know about past cycles to look to the future.

Pluto in Sagittarius, Conjunct to Chiron in Sagittarius

When two planets are in conjunction, they're fused together. It's like having a constant companion, one that never, ever leaves your side. Neither of you ever sees, hears, or experiences anything the other doesn't—and neither of you either acts, or reacts, without the influence of The Other. Turn your gaze first, then, to Pluto and Chiron, dancing cheek-to-cheek at the dawn of The New Millennium, both wearing the sign Sagittarius. Now, Pluto, as we said earlier, is the planet that represents our collective attitude about The Inevitables—Death, Sex, and Regeneration. He's in charge of the gas pedal on The

Evolution Express, and he never looks back. He's also in charge of bringing up the past. He reaches down into our subconscious, collective or otherwise, and pulls up what he knows we've got to face, if we're going to go forward. Sometimes what he sticks in our faces is quite ugly—and sometimes it's beautiful. His job is to dig—to show us what's really inside us, at our core—and to symbolically provide us with the power to make changes by being brutally honest with ourselves. Now, Sagittarius is a costume Pluto isn't quite comfortable wearing. He loves Scorpio best, after all, the sign that's built with enough enduring energy to see the changes he initiates through to the end. Sag, however, while not quite as 'focused' or 'intense' as Scorpio, has a couple of qualities Pluto can work with. First off, Sag is a sign that's quite prophetic, by virtue of its ability to see The Big Picture. Pluto likes that—since he loves having information no one else is privy to. Sag also has an innate hunger Pluto is quite familiar with—a hunger for new experiences. Sag, in fact, has been blessed—and cursed—with Grass Is Greener Syndrome, the never-ending urge to keep going, to keep finding something better, to learn everything there is to learn, and tell it to the world. The symbolic energy of Pluto in Sagittarius, then, conjures the image of a relentless student, poring over reference books by the light of a motel lamp or campfire, stopping briefly to rest along the way of a long journey. Sag never stops traveling, in fact—it's the sign that most loves The Journey, that constantly sets new destinations so that the journey will be endless. This relentless student, then, will be with us throughout the next 1000 years, and will be accompanied by an inseparable companion: Chiron.

Now, on a personal level, Chiron is the place in our charts that shows our 'Sore Spot'—our 'Achilles Heel'. He's the symbolic energy that acts as The Healer, The Wounded One, and The One Who Wounds. Because both are centaurs, many astrologers believe Chiron already has a strong connection with Sag. Personally, I think Chiron's job blends well with Sagittarius because it's up to him to point out What's Wrong—the flaws in the mechanism. While Sagittarius isn't a sign that's world-famous for being detail-conscious, it does give the planet 'wearing' it the ability to laugh about flaws, and to see them philosophically in the context of The Big Picture. So rather than obsessing on what his partner, Pluto, the relentless student, will uncover, Chiron may be able to inspire Pluto to look at the silver lining in the clouds they encounter. The two of them traveling together may be able to share a laugh about the past—with a tear in their eyes—and uncover the magical prescription to heal it. Apply this to 1000 years, and you can see that this combination alone holds the potential to open our collective eyes to What We've Done Wrong to our planet in the most forgiving way possible. Dressed as they both are in benevolent Sag, they don't know what a grudge is —and when you're looking over such Plutonian topics as nuclear waste, war, and pollution, a sense of humor and a forgiving attitude won't hurt.

The Researcher and The Healer

This powerful, penetrating combination of researcher and healer may also see the arrival of The Cure—of many cures, in fact. The catch is that we're going to have to be brutally honest with ourselves about the nature of the disease first—and that hasn't quite happened yet. Although global warming and pollution seem to show up as 'Honorable Mentions' on the political agendas of most politicians vying for The Big Chairs, few have done much to actually put the brakes on. In the United States, this issue is quite hotly debated, since many of the industries we now look to for economic stability go hand-in-hand with perpetuating our environmental problems, rather than putting them to death. Mining digs deep inside the earth, robbing it of its valuables. The destruction of the rainforests has been likened to the destruction of the lungs of the Earth—and to the loss of many plants and organisms that might provide us with the necessary elements for the 'cures' Pluto and Chiron will uncover. (And Chiron is also said to be the first to use plants for medicinal healings.) Since the two will start the New Millennium in a quincunx to Saturn, there's a major adjustment in the Truths We Hold Self-Evident that's going to have to happen before the healing can begin. Saturn will be in Taurus, too—the sign that most allies itself with The Earth, and the sign with the most 'stubborn' reputation out there. In short, the rigid attitudes we've held on to with a white-knuckled grip—and the refusal we've had, up to this point, at least, to even admit there's anything wrong with that attitude—will have to give way to first. We'll have to admit the world is round, that is, before we can ever think of sailing around it.

We'll talk more about Saturn later—but let's go back to Pluto and Chiron, huddled over a text-book, discussing The Heart Of The Matter with unwavering bluntness. Over the last few years, I've noticed that Chiron seems to operate, (mundanely speaking), as our 'Metaphysical Chirurgeon General.' When he traveled through Cancer (the sign of hearth, home, Mom and family ties), our focus turned to maternal, nurturing issues—and the effect of our family upbringing on our adult lives. Psychologists and counselors advertised their services using phrases such as 'healing the dysfunctional family'. It was about that time that we learned, collectively, that nobody's family was perfect—and that not too many of us had a June Cleaver type of Mom. We learned to accept that 'flaw' in our subconscious, and the scar it left on us. We symbolically 'forgave' our Mothers for not being perfect and announced our concern for the well-being of our Earth Mother when Chiron was in Cancer (June 1988-July 1991). The first Earth-Day was held when Chiron was in this sign. Chiron's journey through Leo, which rules procreation and "fathering," (August 1991-August 1993) made 'healing the inner child' the phrase that paid. On the darker side, this passage brought us a whole generation of 'little Chirons'—the children born from the rapes that occurred in Bosnia-Croatia, most of whom were abandoned by their mothers, much as Chiron was—for a similar reason. Within days of Chiron's entry into Virgo, sign of health and hygiene, (August 1993-September 1995), President Clinton brought forth a national health-care plan, describing it in extremely 'Chironic' terms. He said 'Our national health-care system is broken, and it needs to be fixed.' In Libra, the lady with the scales who loves nothing better than Justice, (September 1995-September 1997), Chiron brought us the news that the eco-system was truly 'out of balance'—and that it, too, needed to be fixed. Chiron's tour through Scorpio (September 1997-September 1999), finishing up just a bit before the century does, seems intent on bringing our attention to matters of death, dying, and sexuality (three major Scorpio topics). AIDS, of course, is the first 'symptom' of this passage. Although Pluto is attributed jurisdiction over all 'plagues', especially AIDS, since it's both sexually-transmitted and fatal, Chiron's passage through Pluto's sign brought us the awareness that AIDS is not confined to homosexual men, and that a huge portion of the population of Africa is also HIV-positive. Of course, once again, Pluto and Chiron as a team are a researcher and a healer par excellence—so this conjunction may point to a cure for this horrible disease. On the other hand, if we continue to remain fixed in our refusal to acknowledge the epidemic-proportions at which AIDS is spreading, the inconjunct from Pluto and Chiron to Saturn may have a darker story to tell. Since the first hospitals appeared from 1717 to 1757, most of them during Pluto's last time in Sag (12/1748-11/1762), our deep interest in healing may have an added boost from the establishing of new, state-of-the-art hospitals, equipped with the finest technology, and the finest minds to oversee their use.

The best side of these two united, however, is that they certainly do combine to produce the technology to not only see and understand the problems we're facing as a result of our past abuse of the environment, but also to come up with The Cure. Several colleges (a most Sagittarian group of institutions) have already started work on the project, and Pluto and Chiron may just push it along to a successful end. A program called 'Ecolonomics' has been started through the University of Colorado, to teach young minds how to make environmentalism profitable. Dennis Weaver has pioneered this effort, but his message is catching on.

Education itself seems also to be quite prominently marked in this chart as a key to curing the Earth of what ails her. This makes sense, too—it's lack of education that keeps us ignorant to what's going on around us. Sex education, another fiercely debated topic at the moment, is quite well-described by Pluto in education-hungry Sag—and Chiron's conjunction brings in the hope, once again, of a 'cure', through learning about the causes of the problem. Pluto also brings an 'urgency' to the sign he inhabits—so education in general, and sex-education in particular, seem absolutely necessary if our race is to successfully navigate the 2000's on this relatively tiny planet. Speaking of education, last time out, Pluto's trek through Sag inspired the formation of 7 colleges—Harvard, Columbia, Brown, William and Mary, Yale, Princeton, and Rutgers. I also wonder if education in general won't become more streamlined, with Pluto's fondness of 'cutting to the chase'—that is, if educational institutions won't begin to weed out extraneous classes from degree programs, cutting the time spent in school nearly in half. In a world that's hurrying to educate its inhabitants quickly in specific fields, it strikes me that English majors may not have time to study Physics—and vice versa.

Now, as this century—this Millennium, in fact—is winding up, we're also dealing with two other Plutonian/Chironic topics: abortion and physician-assisted suicide. The latter, in particular, seems relevant to this conjunction, since Chiron was the first physician, the tutor of Asclepius, in fact, and since he also chose to commit suicide rather than continue his life in agony. I see physician-assisted suicide as one of the 'inevitables' we mentioned earlier, in part because the wheels have already started turning towards making it legal, and also since it's a Plutonian issue—and there's no going back on what Pluto starts. Abortion, of course, is something we'll never all agree upon. Unfortunately, although it does involve the decision to terminate a life, this upcoming Millennium's Pluto/Chiron conjunction may also show us the inevitability of the process— especially since we'll also inevitably come face to face with the issue of overpopulation. Sag also rules The Laws we live by, so this may be one of the huge changes this conjunction ushers in: the end to the legal debate, at least.

On the other hand, the researcher and the healer may also come up with more advanced means of birth control, making abortion less of a necessity.

All of those issues—abortion, sex-education, physician-assisted suicide, and overpopulation—are also mentioned in two other places in the chart, through the fact that the Moon, ruler of childbirth, will be in Scorpio, and Ceres, the Mother-Goddess, will be on the Ascendant.

The Religious Right may have their hands full, too, if history repeats itself in another of Sag's departments—religion. Back in 1750, 'The Great Awakening' took place. This New England 'religious revival' came to a screeching halt after colonists forced one Jonathan Edwards to resign his pulpit after growing tired of one too many sermons on 'the sinful nature of mankind.'

Neptune in Aquarius

And then there's Neptune, the pink goddess with the smoke machine and the bucket of pink dust. She's not fond of reality, and isn't above softening the edges, as we talked about earlier. She likes to flip the switch of her magical machine and toss a handful of dust around. The room fills up with pink, fragrant, smoke, and the objects—and people—in it are covered with sparkling dust. Everything is suddenly much, much nicer when she applies her tools—when she glamorizes a situation or an individual—and when she's done, things look better to her. She doesn't have to deal with cold, hard, facts—she can just kick back and dream, munching happily on chocolates while she sits wrapped up in her favorite fuzzy robe, watching love stories on the VCR. Those of us living on the planet during her time in any particular sign, then, are going to experience this famous pink stuff first-hand—courtesy of the qualities that sign represents to us collectively. Now, 'glamour' is the key word here, and to truly understand it, we've got to go back to the days of King Arthur, one of Neptune's favorite time periods. Those were the days—yes, indeed. Makes Neptune sigh just thinking about them. Knights on white horses saved fair maidens from dragons, and chivalry and courtly love abounded. 'Glamour,' at that time, wasn't the title of a teen-magazine, and it had nothing to do with cosmetics or designer fashions. A 'glamour' was a type of spell back then, a spell cast on a person by a wizard or enchantress who wanted to change the appearance of a person, so that they weren't recognizable to others. Of course, as with all spells, the effects were temporary, and eventually the person would revert to their 'real' appearance— but, in the meantime, all kinds of things could happen. The confusion caused by this change of appearance was the reason Arthur arrived. His mother, Igraine, welcomed his father, Uther Pendragon, into her (their, she thought) home, thinking he was her husband, Gorlois—and Arthur was born of their union that night. A magical start to a mythical hero—Neptune's favorite fable. Now, although the meaning of the word 'glamour' has changed, at least on the surface, the effects haven't. She is the enchantress, and when she slips into a sign, it's as if we're collectively falling under a spell of sorts. In others words, we tend to glamorize the qualities associated with this sign—en mass—when the Pink Goddess waves her magic wand over it.

When she first entered Capricorn, for example, we began to idolize the people and the qualities associated with that sign. Capricorn is the sign of the professional, of the leader, of the politician. We certainly have 'deified' our political leaders during this trek, and a number of other leaders, as well. And as long as they didn't behave—openly—in such a way as to allow us to see them clearly and topple them from their pedestals, everything was fine. We adored Ronald Reagan—but weren't quite sure why. We fell in love with our Pope, the most Neptune in Capricorn figure out there, and with preachers, too.

Unfortunately, when these politicians and religious leaders did topple—after the pink stuff eventually shook off, that is— we were forced to see them as they really were, and that's the downside of Neptune's spell. When the smoke clears and we see who and what we've been idolizing as they really are—not as we wanted them to be—we're disappointed. Crushed. So towards the end of Neptune's journey through Capricorn, all kinds of televangelists and politicians, (and even the head of a Neptunian non-profit organization or two), did, indeed topple. Jimmy Swaggart and Jim Baker 'fell from grace', and our President was involved in several scandals, all of which were quite Neptunian in nature. Tax evasion, fraud, secret liaisons.

We also worshipped the qualities of Capricorn—one of which is success. Designer labels sprung up, on everything from bottled water [a wonderful Neptune (water) in Capricorn (walls) image] to underwear. Some folks even bought artificial carphones. In short, we were all captured by the wistful dream Neptune inspired in this sign—captured enough to play into it.

Now, in the chart for the New Millennium, Neptune will be in Aquarius. This is another sign she's not very fond of, but she'll learn to work with it—much like Pluto is, even now, learning to handle Sag. Although her favorite garb is a long, pink, flowing gown—a la Pisces—and Aquarius is much more like a stark white lab-coat—Neptune will come to see that there are some distinct advantages to wearing this costume for a few years. First off, Aquarius believes in her favorite philosophy—that We Are All One. It's a sign that's as unconcerned with age, sex, or religious preference as Neptune is. Aquarius also likes to Spread The Word, and it's the sign that's a veritable computer-wizard—so naturally, Neptune will take advantage of his networking abilities to spread her word.

What's she going to look like, dressed in Aquarius? Well, picture a Goddess in a lab coat, wandering around a computer laboratory, running her fingers over the keys to each and every machine, smiling as she imagines all the wonderful magic she can bring to the world with what she knows now. One of her main jobs, remember, is to provide us with 'Altered States'—to give us 'escape hatches' from the world when reality becomes too much for us. Although her favorite tools are usually sleep, drugs, alcohol, television, religion, and dreams, with computers she'll be able to create amazing 'escapes.' We won't have to drink, smoke, or ingest them, either. Just pushing the PC on will do it. We've already started work on some of what will be her pet projects, too—Virtual Reality, the ultimate 'computer fantasy,' is just the beginning—but it's a damned good one.

Imagine entering a world of your own creation, and being able to walk around inside it—all from the comfort of your living room. Imagine falling in love with someone—dreamily, Neptunianly sighing over someone—that you've only 'met' over a keyboard. It's already happened—it's called 'internet romance,' and although it began with Neptune in Capricorn, Neptune in Aquarius will turn the volume way, way up. We'll be 'bonding' with others through the thoughts we share, rather than any actual physical attractions. Without the 'hindrance' of physical appearance to hold us back, we'll be connecting with folks we never would've imagined ourselves interested in at all. Of course, the downside of Neptune's symbolism still applies—so we still stand to be a bit disappointed with our fantasies if and when we try to make them into reality. In other words, actually seeing someone, even after hours of intimate letter-writing, may shatter the fantasy, and bring us down to earth with a crash.

Of course, computer viruses are perfectly described by the assembling Neptune/Aquarius keywords, and I think we'll have to deal with a lot more of those, too. Neptune rules the hidden and the invisible and is in charge of the viruses that infiltrate our bodies' immune systems. Aquarius is the sign that's in charge of computers and new technologies. Her presence in this sign also accounts for the fear of many computer experts that when the year 2000 arrives, our computer systems won't be able to handle the change without mega-confusion which could lead to a complete and total crash of all systems, too. This possibility is heightened since Uranus will be in Aquarius, too, as 2000 rolls around, and in a square to Saturn, the ruler of Time. The combination of these factors also point to the fact that all our computer systems will be quite 'vulnerable' when Neptune enters this new sign, intent as she often is on breaking down or dissolving barriers.

Neptune's jurisdiction over fashion will be interesting to watch, too, as she enters the hallowed halls of Donna Karan and other designers and begins to feel a bit too restricted in those neat, tidy Capricorn threads.

In Aquarius, her tastes will tend towards the eclectic, to say the very least—and I think we're going to be quite surprised at what it suddenly becomes 'fashionable' to wear. Aquarius is quite androgynous, for starters, so I'll bet we'll see a lot more intermingling of styles previously created and worn by only one sex. Again, 1000 years is a long, long time, and it's tough to imagine what we'll be decked out in by the time even a quarter of it has passed, but you can count on Individuality being much more important to folks than dressing like the Joneses.

Now, this lady also symbolically influences a generation's attitudes on drugs, alcohol, and religion. So once she enters Aquarius, we'd all better fasten our seat belts and put our table-trays in the 'up' position—especially those of us who have rather Puritan views on these subjects. Although it sounds like a stretch—right now, at least—to imagine marijuana ever being legalized, for example, it seems inevitable in the not-so-distant future, with the Goddess of Altered States in free-wheeling Aquarius. The sign's affinity with the laboratory alone will bring its legalization for medical purposes, at least, and that, too, is already in motion. Not to mention that every news magazine cover features a story on 'The New Psychedelic Drugs' (laboratory-manufactured, of course) at least once a month. The complete turnarounds inspired by Aquarius, of course, could also mean that our attitudes about presently used drugs, like alcohol and nicotine, will be the first to go. Neptune's trek through strict Capricorn tightened up the reins on smokers and drinkers, and I expect to see that continue.

Since Aquarius represents the scientist, it's also going to be interesting to see what type of pharmaceutical drugs arise, to aid Pluto and Chiron in their search for 'cures' to previously fatal diseases. Will we have new drugs to help AIDS sufferers live? Will cancer become obsolete? It's all quite possible—quite probable, really—once Neptune, the planet with an endless well of compassion, is set loose in the lab. And speaking of compassionate labs, let's all hope that science finally sees the light about the cruelty of testing unnecessary products on animals. Last time she was in this sign, anesthetics (scientific 'escapes' from the pain of surgical procedures) like chloroform and ethyl ether were first used—back in 1842.

Now, Neptune also rules films—movies, that is—because they recreate the world through the fantasy of a director's eyes. Neptune in Aquarius sounds like a new 'trend' developing towards heroines, rather than heroes, in our movies—and that's already begun, too. Consider Jodie Foster's part as an astronomer who finds her way to Vega in *Contact*, and Sigourney Weaver's space-heroine character in *Alien Ressurection*. Rather than 'shoot-em-ups,' I think our tastes in entertainment will turn towards the scientific and the space-oriented. Only thing is, with Uranus also in Aquarius as the galactic speedometer rolls over, I have a hunch that space—at least, our galaxy's part of it—may no longer be the final frontier, and sci-fi writers will be hard-pressed to come up with anything that's going to beat what's going to be real. Neptune's upcoming visit has already been heralded by the release of *Amistad*, too—an event which took place in July of 1839, the last time she sailed through the sign of the seafarer. Remember, although Aquarius is an air sign, its name means 'Water-Bearer', and its glyph is ocean waves. Aquarius has everything to do with ships— 'bearers' of people and objects 'over water.' Her last visit through this sign made rowing and sailing quite popular sports—a trend which really set in around 1843, and brought with it a new type of entertainment on water—the Showboats, which made their debuts back in the 30's. Her ability to symbolically incite rebellions of underdogs, in her Aquarian costume, also brought about another mutiny of slaves at sea, 'The Creole Incident', which occurred on October 27, 1841. Look for that event to be made into a film over the next few years, too. Since The Alamo also occurred during her last visit to Aquarius—and with Aquarius's propensity to create striking representations of the past, this, too, may be made into a new, more realistic film chronicle, as may the journey of the Cherokees over the infamous 'Trail of Tears' (December, 1838).

With Neptune as the ruler of fluids, and especially the Mother of all Waters, the ocean, I also wonder if the predicted long-term effects of El-Nino aren't also receiving an Honorable Mention in this chart. The sudden changes and radical behavior associated with Aquarius could certainly extend to the behavior of our oceans. Along with the quincunx between Pluto/ Chiron and Saturn, this could also point to radical earth-changes that include new continents. Not quite so far-fetched when you consider that the Uranus-Neptune conjunction in Capricorn re-arranged the lines on the maps quite well, bringing down the barrier between East and West Germany, making the USSR into a mass of countries, and turning the former Yugoslavia into a battle between Bosnians and Crotians. Capricorn represents boundaries—and Neptune in Capricorn, with an assist from sudden Uranus, brought home the point that imagined lines on a piece of paper do not a 'real' boundary make—even if millions of world citizens bought into the facade.

Probably the most important thing about Neptune's position in this chart has to do with her conjunction to the South Node, however. In any chart, the nodes represent the intersection of two 'Great Circles'—the Sun's apparent orbit around the Earth and the Moon's real orbit. The North Node is a signpost of sorts that points towards the future—the South

Node shows the past. Any planet to the south Node urges us to take the best of what we know from past history to push toward the future. With a planet as potent—although subtle—as Neptune in alliance with the South Node, then, the message is clear. We can't allow the lies we've told ourselves in the past to interfere with what lies ahead. The challenge will be to incorporate our Neptunian visions from the past—again, via sci-fi, technological works in progress, etc.—to create a better world. Not unimportantly, Neptune will also be in sextile to Venus in Sagittarius as the Millennium begins, bringing together the pink goddess and her compatriot in an exciting, Other-oriented fire/air aspect that seems to ensure that our compassion will extend past our personal relationships to include Everyone. This aspect could also be translated to mean that racism will be gone—but not through another Civil War. Neptune's magical ability to blend and infiltrate, connected to Venus in Sag's love of foreign places and people, suggests that there may only be one 'race' by the time this 1000 period ends. Talk about an evolutionary step that's been subtly engineered—as we gradually mix and intermarry, we'll be blending everything about our race, both physical and spiritual. That's one to keep our fingers crossed about.

Uranus in Aquarius

Our third stop is to Uranus, also in Aquarius, who won't have to do any adapting at all to get used to the new costume change. He'll have been in this sign for a few years by the time The New Millennium arrives, a sign he'd been waiting anxiously to re-inhabit for 77 years—since he last left his favorite threads behind to enter Pisces, back in 1920. Since this is the sign he operates most freely in, the sign that most cooperates with his need to discover, invent, and Fight City Hall, his symbolic influence on this new era will be quite potent. Remember, this is the guy who is the Mad Scientist, the prototype that inspired the professor in *Back To The Future*—and if you'll remember, he was the inventor of a machine that allowed the movie's hero to time-travel. What does he look like, in Aquarius? Well, picture a frozen ice-God, staring into the future with frozen ice-blue eyes, topped off with Andy Rooney eyebrows. There are icicles hanging from those brows, and from his long silver beard, too. His hair is also silver, and quite unruly. He wears a stark white robe that crackles when he walks, like a sheet that's been left out on the clothesline too long in February—his favorite month. In this guise, although he does appear to be quite mad, his potential for genius is unsurpassed. This white Aquarian outfit allows him to trash everything he's ever learned from the past with one wave of his cold, white hand—in order to create the future. He's not fond of rules—only of breaking them. It's a good thing that someone does break rules, however—or no one would ever try a new technique, experiment with something that's previously been seen as 'crazy', or rebel against an unfair Authority Figure. He's not a bit afraid of what will happen if he doesn't conform—in fact, he loves to be different, to be seen in Their eyes as radical. It's what he lives for.

In Aquarius, he'll set to work accelerating science, space travel, and computer technology—his Departments, that is—at a speed we won't be able to believe. Neptune's whispered dreams from just a few degrees back will inspire him to Create The Technology that will make the recent past look like the Stone Age. Last time he inhabited this sign, after all, he helped Ford to invent the auto assembly-line, (Summer, 1913), talked Margaret Sanger into opening the first birth-control clinic, (1916), and sat in with Alexander Graham Bell while he put through the first transcontinental phone call (1/25/1915) . He was also in the neighborhood when the Victrola arrived (1915), and the first 'airmail' deliveries were made (1918). The time before that, (1828-1835), he inspired the Age of the Railroad, with the opening of the B&O (Baltimore and Ohio) on 7/4/1828. He didn't forget urban travel, either—the first streetcar whirred into life with his Aquarian help (11/26/1832), and he talked a Vermont blacksmith, Thomas Davenport, into developing the prototype of the electric motor. The first books on one of Uranus's favorite topics, Political Science, were also published. Quite the resumé.

This time out, he's delighted to find that Things have already begun stretching toward even more futuristic inventions. And just imagine what this computer-savvy guy will help us to create. The internet was already up and running when he returned home to Aquarius, but his input helped the World Wide Web to really take off. The Information Superhighway stands ready to unite us all with the touch of a keypad, too—but there's so much more. Any issue of *Discover* or *Scientific American* or *Omni* provides glimpses of what he's got up his sleeve this time 'round, and it's stupefying. How about a credit-card that isn't really a credit-card—it's a personal record of Everything You Always Wanted To Know About You. Your social security number, driver's license, charge cards, bank accounts—everything. Conveniently encapsulated on a small plastic card. How about voice-activated locks and car ignitions? And imagine if that voice did more than tell you your lights were on—it told you how to get where you were going, complete with AAA-like travel advisories. It's all up the road—literally. Think computers are everywhere now? Imagine what it will be like in 50, or 100—or 1000 years. HAL[1] may have company coming.

Communication will necessarily be phenomenal—perhaps even phenomenal enough to put us in touch with Them—the others. Although we haven't found anyone to chat with here in our own universe, there are billions of other star systems to dial up—perhaps *Contact* isn't science fiction at all. Sit down and watch *The Fifth Element* if you really want to get a feeling for what it will be like to 'drive' in a lane that's seven or eight stories above the ground—and to have Chinese food delivered via the restaurant itself, as it hovers outside your window, a dozen floors up. What's so outrageous, then, about this ultra-communicator in his most long-winded sign, handing us the phone and saying 'It's for you. Vega calling.' What about extra-terrestrials coming to visit? Well, some say they already have—but Uranus isn't much on secrets, and although Pluto is, his Sag costume never did inspire a planet to keep a secret very well. So if there's going to be contact made by Them, I don't see it as being a secret at all.

Will we actually inhabit other planets? Well, if it were my call, I'd say You Betcha, with Uranus sitting as the focal point of a Moon/Saturn opposition. In fact, my money would be on the Moon as our first Space-Condo site. The Moon in Scorpio opposite to Saturn in Taurus certainly does point to living in a

---

[1] from *2001: A Space Odyssey*

super-controlled environment—perhaps even a super-controlled atmosphere. I don't think it's any accident that Mars lies very close to the position of the Moon in the US chart[2] (pick one—they're all in Aquarius), so that, too, may be a place we set down stakes—but still, the Moon does represent Home, and Security, astrologically-speaking, and having her this tight with Uranus, the creator of What You'd Never Be Able To Imagine, and Saturn, The Reality-Maker, certainly sounds like a Home On Another Planet. My fondest hope is that we don't ignore Pluto/Chiron's issues long enough to make a global migration a necessity. It would be ever so much nicer to go because it was exciting, not because we had strangled our own lovely home with pollutants.

The Rest of the Story....

Of course, all the planets in any chart are important to consider. After all, leaving Saturn out of any chart delineation is just asking for trouble, and if Mars isn't invited, he'll crash the party. So let's look at the rest of them, briefly—so there won't be any hurt feelings up there on Mt. Olympus.

Saturn in Taurus, Retrograde

Now, here's the planet that's long been associated with The Authorities. Think of him as Ichobod Crane, that schoolmaster of *Legend of Sleepy Hollow* fame, a very stern, very gaunt, unsmiling gentleman who's only too happy to shake a finger at naughty students. He's the ultimate Nay-Sayer, the gentleman with the perpetual scowl who only sees the pessimistic side of things. On the other hand, Saturn is also conjured quite nicely by imagining an Indian grandmother, wise and serious, who holds us back when we're about to act too quickly. Saturn has a bad reputation, inspired by a love of caution, restraint, and Just Saying No—but without this planet's symbolic urges, we'd fall apart. Saturn is in charge of the structure of all things—the backbone in the human body, the main beams in a building, the frame of an automobile, the leaders that form the foundation of a nation.

---

[2] Astrological Inside Joke: Although most astrologers agree our country was "born" on July 4, 1776, the exact time is unknown, so many different charts are competing for the honor of "US Birthchart." However, the Moon does occupy Aquarius in each and every one of the competing US Charts.

In Taurus, he's a bit more fixed in his pessimism, impossible to talk into budging at all, once he's made a decision. Picture him as an old-time preacher, doling out hellfire from his pulpit, telling one and all to refrain from everything. As one of the representatives of The Religious Right, (along with Pluto in Sag), his retrograde motion, long a chart-indicator of an entity without a strong 'father-figure,' may show the last death-throes of a movement that's bent on taking us backwards, rather than into the future. Without a leader that's 'worth his weight,' (a favorite Taurus ideal), and quite reputable, they may finally see the necessity for loosening up on their hold to the past so that the future can unfold. Remember, Saturn in Taurus is a very, very rigid archetype—it's like a building that's been constructed without the benefit of an inch or two of 'give' in the event of an earthquake. Add the fact that Uranus is in a square to Saturn in this chart, and there's just that brewing—an 'earthquake' en route that could shake and shatter any institutions whose leaders are too rigid. This square also points to an 'argument' of sorts, one we're quite familiar with —over holding on stolidly to the past vs. moving quickly along into the future. Uranus has seen walls, of course—and he knows how easily they tumble. Any institutions that aren't built with a bit of allowance for change will certainly come crashing down when Uranus grabs them at the roots and shakes, then.

With Saturn retrograde, it's also a good bet that the Pluto/ Chiron conjunction that's quincunx to it will show us the error in what we previously believed—in many departments. Government has always been associated with Saturn—in Venus' sign, the problem will undoubtedly have to do with money. Whether it's taxes or political salaries, something's going to give—suddenly—when Uranus takes hold of the money-belt and reveals its contents to all.

Jupiter in Aries, Mars in Aquarius

Here's our favorite uncle, dressed in a uniform. He's an enforcer with a twinkle in his eye, the Irish Cop with the substantial belly in all the old movies. Now, Jupiter doesn't have a great deal of patience to start with. He hates to wait, and he hates to be told he can't do anything—anything at all. In Aries, he'll be a bit less likely to stop himself, and much more apt to keep going, once he's got acceleration.

His rulership over education, again, is an indication of 'streamlining.' As impatient as he'll be for results, all our colleges and universities may turn into the modern equivalent of The Trade School, teaching students only what they need to know to succeed in their chosen fields, rather than having them complete years' worth of courses that aren't connected to the goal.

Jupiter, of course, also rules The Law, so it wouldn't surprise me at all if, in his Aries red, he decides that it's time to create laws that are contemporary—more suited to the people we've become, that is, as opposed to the people we were when those laws were written. I'd imagine this placement would also point to a much tougher stance on punishment—Jupiter, after all, is a benevolent dictator, but a dictator, nonetheless.

Jupiter's love of travel combined with Aries' red urgency also combines to produce a traveler in a hurry— and as eager as Uranus will be to show off his Aquarian talents, it's a given that all 'long-distance travel' won't take as long as it did. Trains, jets, and planes will be super-fast. In fact, the only 'long-trips' that remain, time-wise, at least— may be trips to Aries' planet: Mars. Jupiter's connection by stimulating sextile to Mars may also add fuel to our fire, to actually visit The Red Planet—or, again, to set up camp there. With Mars also in Aquarius, it certainly sounds as if traveling to this planet will be made possible through advanced electronics and computers. In an aspect as energetic as the sextile, it's also a given that the Aquarian discoveries and advancements of the New Millennium will move along much more quickly than we can comprehend at this time. Mars, of course, also rules law enforcement—the officers who actually slap the handcuffs on the bad-guys, that is. So Mars in this computer-oriented sign may just mean that our law enforcement officials (finally) create an efficient network—to help each other apprehend criminals across state—and international—boundaries. It may also point to the need for tighter controls on The Internet— which has already been shown. Since Aquarius is far more cold and clear-minded than warm and fuzzy, it's a good bet we'll be dealing with criminals in a much 'colder' way.

Venus in Sagittarius

And what about The Lovely Lady Venus, wearing a Sagittarian outfit? What kind of picture does this create? Well, here's the international (and possibly interplanetary) ambassador, ready to spread tidings of good will to one and all. Boundaries were never a problem for Sagittarius, after all. This is the sign that loves to take its act on the road. Positioned as she is in a sextile to her 'big sister' Neptune, in the two most open-minded signs out there, it looks like our views of what's 'acceptable' relationship-wise also stand to broaden, world-wide.

Prejudice will become obsolete—or very unacceptable—in this new age. Once again, with Neptune's talent for blending, this may be due to the fact that we'll have cross-bred so many times that at the end of the next 1000 years there will only be one race—and no one to be prejudiced against. In any event, taking Sag's love of 'foreigners' and Aquarius's fondness for What's Unusual certainly adds up to an acceptance of all types of partnerships.

Venus' jurisdiction over money, Sag's love of incorporation, and Neptune's boundary-dissolving abilities also indicates that there may be only one form of currency in the far-off future—no 'money' at all. It's not too much of a stretch to think of money becoming useless—think of what we've already achieved with Direct Deposits, ATM cards, and computerized 'checks.' And wouldn't that be a great boon for the trees?

Mercury in Capricorn
Mercury in Capricorn
Mercury in Capricorn

Now, there's no sign out there that loves repetition as much as Capricorn. So let's turn our thoughts to the issue of cloning—of 'repeating' genetic structures. Of course, that's already started— 'Dolly' was the first of many living 'repetitive structures.' Although there's a ban on cloning humans now in effect, it strikes me that it won't last long. Science never was very good at applying the brakes once it made a discovery it found astounding, and cloning certainly does fall into that category.

There's also an 'official' mindset that Mercury uses when he's decked out in Capricorn—a 'tightening-up' that happens when this ordinarily fleet-footed God dresses in Capricorn pinstripes. What could that mean? Well, first of all, it may mean that all our communications carry a 'Just The Facts, Ma'am' quality that eliminates all but the most pertinent of facts. There's no embellishments with Capricorn, and that may mean that our friends in The Media will need to cut back on the sensational to deliver just what's real. This doesn't look good for tabloids, of course, but we may have already seen the demise of the popularity the tabs have had—since the death of the much-loved Princess of Wales brought a touch of conscience (and the question of how much responsibility the ravenous public should assume) to our Enquiring Little Minds. It's a sure bet that most of us will be less interested in sit-coms and far more interested in Facts, once this New Millennium kicks in.

The Sun in Capricorn, Trine To Saturn—And 'Longevity'.....

With the Sun in Capricorn, in a trine to Saturn in immovable Taurus, it also looks like we're going to live longer—a lot longer. Taurus hates change—it holds on tight to whatever it owns. With Saturn in so stubborn a sign, in trine to the Sun, the life-force, in Saturn's sign, then, we'll be holding on tightly to our lives. Now, if we're living quality lives, that's going to be wonderful—and with the medical breakthroughs Uranus in his own sign certainly portends, it looks as if that's a distinct possibility. If we also pay attention to the problem of Overpopulation, and take steps to prolong life well, rather than keep creating more and more citizens of the planet to eat up her resources, this could point to a race with an eye on Quality, rather than Quantity. Both Saturn and Capricorn also never take more than they need—so there may be very, very small families in our future.

Juno in Capricorn on The IC...

Add Juno, the asteroid of committed relationships, just three degrees away from the Sun, and it's also easy to speculate that our marriages stand to last longer and be far more 'independent' in nature. This placement, in fact, says an awful lot about 'childless couples.' I don't see a trend for 'open-marriages' or polygamy arising from this placement, that's for sure. With

Juno positioned as she is at the very base of the chart, the IC from which all else operates, this principle will be very, very important to all humanity, as will the qualities of Respecting Our Elders and Learning From Our Mistakes.

Vesta in Sagittarius...

Vesta, of course, is the asteroid that represents an awe for what's sacred. In Sag, she's prophetic and able to see the Big Picture. Placed as she is between Pluto/Chiron and Venus, she may bring us an understanding of how important it is to recycle our resources—if we're going to make the long haul through another 1000 years. Vesta may also point to a respect for all religions, or more 'blending' of the concept of What's Holy.

Ceres in Libra on the Ascendant...

Now, here's the asteroid goddess of nurturing, the one that speaks of food, and agriculture. Her position in Libra asks that we restore balance to the planet through sharing food, cooperative use of food, and partnerships involving production and distribution of food. An end to hunger? Well, we can certainly hope....

Pallas Athena Opposite Uranus, Trine Pluto/Chiron, Square Saturn and The Moon...

We end our tour of The New Millennium with a stop at Pallas Athena, who's quite involved with several 'heavy-hitters' in this chart. In Leo, she champions her heroes valiantly, and in the type of fixed cross she finds herself in, she'll have her hands full. Still, although she'll be involved in the population struggle and the colonization of other planets, her trine to Pluto/Chiron shows that what will come easiest for her will be to champion Change, Healing, and Cures to social ills. In Leo, she may speak of the role our entertainers will play in accomplishing these ends. In the past, performers like Sting and Willie Nelson have put their celebrity status to fine use, championing causes for the benefit of certain groups and causes. Her position here looks to be a continuation of that trend.

What About The US In Particular?

Now, no matter which chart you use for the US, we still have some idea of how this new era will pan out, both through what we've just discussed, with reference to the moment of January 1st, 2000, 12:00 AM, but also through the transits the US chart will be receiving at the moment the New Millennium arrives.

- The Moon in Scorpio will trine our Sun/Jupiter/Venus conjunction in Cancer. This may mean that we take the lead in the issue of Population Control—something that seems to have already been put into action through our leadership at Population Summits already held.

- Mercury in Capricorn will oppose our Venus/Jupiter. Will we be funding cloning research—or opposing it? Will we be the first nation to tire of the sensational in our news? The first to tighten up on fact vs. fiction in our expectations from The Media?

- Venus in Sag will oppose our Uranus, and quincunx our Venus. This may mean that we're the nation that will need to do the most 'adjustment' to become involved in a global currency—which also seems quite accurate. Remember, there's a 'language problem' between two planets in quincunx—they have nothing to 'talk about', since they don't share an element, a gender, or a quality. We've already started work on the New Millennium's blending of race, of course. There's no other country that's composed of quite so many nationalities—or that's had to make so many 'adjustments' to accommodate a variety of languages, traditions, and religions.

- Mars in Aquarius will conjoin with our Moon, and trine our Mars. This is a big one—and it sounds as if we'll continue to be the strongest country in the world, as far as armed forces and defense capabilities go. It may also point to the world viewing us as The Aggressors, however—and with Mars on the Moon, we may continue to be the victims of attacks from within our own citizenry.

- Jupiter will square our Mercury and our Pluto, forming the apex of a T-square. Translated literally, we may be the focus of many international conflicts—but what's new? We may also be forced to learn other languages, (instead of expecting the rest of the world to learn ours) if we're to continue to keep leadership of 'the blending process.'

- Saturn, the only planet that will be retrograde, will sextile our Jupiter/Sun. We'll definitely be the leaders in the search for ways to live longer, more fulfilling lives.

- Uranus will be separating from a trine to our Uranus, edging towards a trine to Mars, and in an exact trine to our Saturn. This points to our leadership in Science and Warfare, and may even show that we're the model the rest of the world will look to for an example of how to make positive changes that serve as a foundation for a realistic future.

- Neptune will be coming up to a conjunction with our south node, then trining our Uranus—and the nodal axis at the turn of The New Millennium will be just 3 degrees away from a conjunction to our own. This is a powerful statement about just how much we'll need to be on guard against viruses (human and computerized) and chemical warfare. It's also a positive statement about the continuing need for the US to extend a compassionate hand to the rest of the world, and it speaks of just how 'commonplace' computer technology will be among citizens of our country. This isn't too far-fetched, either—how many of us have PC's we use on a daily basis?

- Pluto/Chiron will oppose our Uranus, and sextile our Saturn. If Pluto/Chiron represents the need to find Cures, the sextile to our Saturn certainly indicates that we'll take responsibility for that task. The opposition to our Uranus means that we may need to join in partnerships with other nations to accomplish that goal.

In short, there are all kinds of connections between the dawn of this momentous era and the US chart. Fortunately, the MC degree at 0 AM on January 1st of every year in Washington is 7 Cancer—which puts our Jupiter on it. This seems to be a long-term blessing, but the Ascendant degree at that same moment every year puts our Saturn in the first house, just 8-9 degrees away from the 'Front Door,' and indicates that our responsibility to the rest of the planet is a permanent one. It seems, then, that if we can continue to balance Growth with Caution and Discipline, we'll retain our status in the world community, and keep our nation alive and well.

And, In Conclusion.....

Well, the good news is that all the 'hype' about the world ending when the planetary speedometer rolls over is just that. There's a great deal of future promised here. There are new discoveries, societal changes, and even geographic shifts mentioned. Of course, the fact that the Moon will be in Scorpio at this moment also may lead the pessimists among us to conclude that the world won't last another 1000 years—but I beg to differ. Scorpio only seeks to initiate complete and total change—from the bottom up. It's the sign that most reflects Pluto's love of clearing the decks to afford new life the room to take hold—but Death is only a last resort. If we allow ourselves to make those huge, sweeping changes, as a race, the planet will continue with the process of Life, Death, and Rebirth that Scorpio and Pluto really represent.

All kidding aside, if you're one of the lucky ones that's going to be here when the New Millennium arrives, consider how these planetary placements will touch your own chart—and think about what a tremendous gift it is to be on the planet as this new century unfolds. Use your life—and your transits at this moments, then—as a tool to help the world with the new planetary activity that will be hovering over all of us. Life is a journey, and as such, you've got options. Putting your own unique bundle of energy to work in the best way possible—for yourself, and for all of us—is the best way to add positive energy to the planet's collective path.

PLANETARY ALIGNMENTS AND OTHER MYTHS

One of the basic principles of the astrological study of cycles is: the more rare an astrological configuration is, the more it is likely to be significant. The corollary is: the more common a particular astrological pattern is, the less significant it is likely to be. A number of people who are not versed in planetary cycles have given much too much importance to certain celestial events. They talk about "alignments" as if they were exceedingly rare occurrences when, in astronomical fact, most of the ballyhooed alignments are rather common.

A case in point is the "alignment" which is expected in May 5th of the year 2000. Some people have suggested it signals the onset of one of Nostradamus' Armageddon prophecies. The "special alignment" was even central to an episode on a TV show (*Millennium*). Yet, the actual "alignment" on May 5th of 2000 consists of only five planets within a 20-degree arc of the zodiac. Such alignments have occurred many times in history. In the year 2000, a planetary cluster of five or more planets within a 20-degree arc occurs on April 30th , May 2nd, May 3rd, May 5th, May 16th, June 1st and June 16th. (On May 3, 2000, in fact, seven planets will be in the sign of Taurus, but they will be separated by about 26 degree. By May 5th, both Mars and the Moon will have moved from Taurus into Gemini.) In the

20th century, there were only six years which did **not** have a collection of five planets within a 20-degree arc! Most years had such planetary clusters several times. Between January 1, 1700 and December 31, 2050, there were 1562 occurrences of 5 or more planets being within a 20-degree arc. (This data is taken from *Tables of Planetary Phenomena* by Neil F. Michelsen.)

You can break those 1562 occurrences in the following sub-sets:

Combinations	Number	Average Time
5 planets with the Moon	1093	1 day, 9 hours, 46 minutes
5 planets without the Moon	303	12 days, 17 hours, 33 minutes
6 planets with the Moon	128	1 day, 8 hours, 52 minutes
6 planets without the Moon	28	8 days, 8 hours, 23 minutes
7 planets with the Moon	8	1 day, 15 hours, 56 minutes
7 planets without the Moon	2	3 days, 18 hours, 47 minutes

Naturally, when the Moon was part of a planetary clusters, the amount of time that the cluster existed was shorter, due to the more rapid speed of the Moon.

As noted above, there were 10 times (between 1700 and 2050) in which clusters of 7 planets were formed (or will form) within a 20-degree arc of the zodiac. The following table (from *Tables of Planetary Phenomena* by Neil F. Michelsen) lists the dates for those ten occasions. It also provides the time when the 20-degree arc of planets began, and the zodiac position of the first planet in the sequence. The duration of the cluster is given—in days, hours, and minutes. The date and time of the ending of the cluster is also provided, along with the first planet in the sequence when the cluster is phasing out. The planets are provided in zodiacal sequence for the both the beginning and the ending of the cluster period.

Based on rarity, we would highlight the years 1762, 1821 (which had three occurrences of planetary clusters within a 20-degree arc), 1831, 1850, 1882, 1962, 1994, and 2032. In terms of history, 1831 was a time of economic panic in the United

Ten Occurrences of 7 Planets Clustered within a 20° Arc

	Starting Position		Planets in Zodiacal Sequence	Dy Hr Mn	Ending Position		Planets in Zodiacal Sequence
1762	Mar 24 18:04	23♓48	☽ ☿ ♀ ☉ ♅ ♄ ♃	1 19 29	Mar 26 13:33	26♓28	☿ ♀ ☉ ♅ ♄ ♃ ☽
1821	Apr 1 5:26	21♓10	☽ ♂ ♀ ♇ ☿ ♃ ☉	1 13 34	Apr 2 19:00	24♓57	♂ ♇ ☿ ♀ ♃ ☉ ☽
1821	Apr 1 12:53	25♓51	☽ ♀ ♇ ☿ ♃ ☉ ♄	1 11 51	Apr 3 0:44	28♓36	♇ ☿ ♀ ♃ ☉ ♄ ☽
1821	Apr 4 10:07	26♓13	♂ ☿ ♇ ♀ ♃ ☉ ♄	3 2 10	Apr 7 12:16	27♓21	☿ ♂ ♇ ♀ ♃ ♄ ☉
1831	Jan 13 22:38	21♑33	☽ ♆ ☉ ♃ ♀ ♅ ☿	1 15 11	Jan 15 13:49	22♑34	♆ ☉ ♃ ♀ ♅ ☿ ☽
1850	Apr 11 17:24	11♈27	☽ ♄ ☿ ☉ ♅ ♇ ♀	0 16 28	Apr 12 9:52	12♈17	♄ ☿ ☽ ☉ ♅ ♇ ♀
1882	May 3 0:20	12♉27	☉ ☿ ♄ ♆ ♇ ♀ ♃	4 11 23	May 7 11:43	15♉49	♄ ♆ ☉ ☿ ♇ ♃ ♀
1962	Feb 3 20:16	28♑20	☽ ♂ ♄ ☉ ♀ ☿ ♃	1 15 5	Feb 5 11:20	2♒44	♂ ♄ ☉ ☿ ♀ ♃ ☽
1994	Jan 10 17:06	4♑29	☽ ♂ ♀ ☉ ♆ ♅ ☿	2 12 43	Jan 13 5:49	18♑27	♂ ♆ ♀ ♅ ☉ ☿ ☽
2032	Jun 7 19:54	14♊49	☽ ☉ ♀ ♄ ♅ ♂ ☿	1 23 3	Jun 9 18:56	19♊29	☉ ♀ ♄ ♅ ♂ ☿ ☽

The first zodiacal position shown is the position of the first planet in the sequence which is listed in zodiacal order. The time span or duration that the planets remain within the 20° arc is shown as days, hours and minutes. The second zodiacal position is that of the first planet in the sequence when the planets are about to leave the 20° arc. Again, the planets are shown in zodiacal order.

Looking at the first entry in the above table, one sees the Moon as the leading planet in the entry sequence. One day, 19 hours and 29 minutes later the Moon has passed the other 6 planets to become the trailing planet and the one to break the 20° cluster of this grouping.

States. The Cuban Missile Crisis highlighted 1962 and a major earthquake in the Los Angeles area was featured in 1994. The cluster of 2032 occurs in the sign of Gemini, suggesting significant developments are likely to involve communication, the dissemination of information, media, transportation, or intellectual matters. We could project anything from extraterrestrial contact, to a breakthrough in transportation, to major media changes, to significant alterations in the educational system or the ways people process data.

Looking backward first allows us to be wiser in our future projections. Aftere identifying patterns which are truly rare, we can pay attention to them. By correlating current patterns with past events and cycles, we have a better idea of what to expect. Astrologically, the year 2000 is not a major one.

Appendix

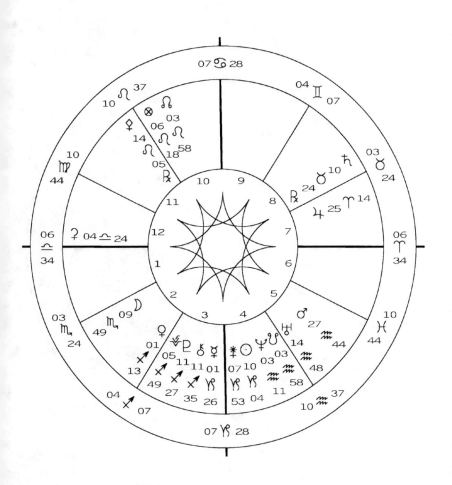

Chart for Washington, D. C.
January 1, 2000

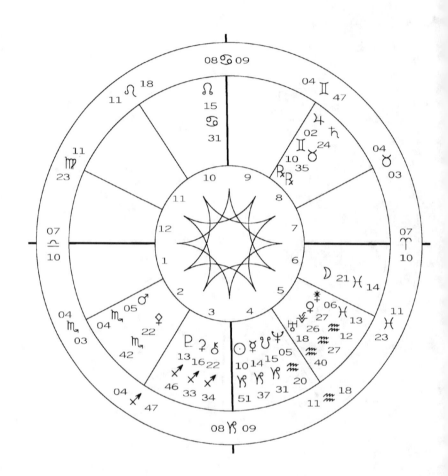

Chart for Washington, D. C.

January 1, 2001

Planetary Placements for U. S. Chart

Sun	13 Cancer
Moon	17 -29 Aquarius
Mercury	24 Cancer ℞
Venus	2 Cancer
Mars	21 Gemini
Jupiter	5 Cancer
Saturn	14 Libra
Uranus	8 Gemini
Neptune	22 Virgo
Pluto	27 Capricorn ℞
Ceres	8 Pisces ℞
Pallas	26 Aquarius ℞
Juno	20 Libra
Vesta	19 Taurus
Chiron	20 Aries
No. Node	6 Leo
So. Node	6 Aquarius

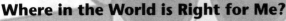